FOOLIN' A ...NITY

BY

Steven Dietz

SAMUEL FRENCH, INC.
45 WEST 25TH STREET   NEW YORK 10010
7623 SUNSET BOULEVARD   HOLLYWOOD 90046
LONDON   *TORONTO*

for Leslie

IMPORTANT BILLING AND CREDIT REQUIREMENTS

"When informed that the Shelter is full,
close the entrance and do <u>NOT</u> allow
additional people to enter.

Sufficient shelter is available for the
entire population if properly distributed."

> Card Number 2.
> Item Number 6.
> Fallout Shelter Emergency Instructions
> United States Department of Civil
>   Defense.

"These are days of lasers in the jungle,
lasers in the jungle somewhere.
Staccato signals of constant information,
a loose affiliation
of millionaires and billionaires."

> Paul Simon
> "The Boy in the Bubble"

"God, look at her. She doesn't even have a *tan*."

> Overheard on a beach in Connecticut, 1986.

Foolin' Around With Infinity was presented by Brass Tacks Theatre in Minneapolis from November 4th to December 11th, 1988.

The set was designed by Lori Lynne Sullivan, lights by Michael Murnane, costumes by Katherine Maurer. The stage manager was Stacey M. Scanlan. The production was directed by the author.

The cast was as follows:

ARTHUR "MAC" McCORMICK
.... Richard Arthur Erickson
JOHN "JESSE" RANDALL......... Dane Stauffer
LUKE .... Sally Wingert
MR. ANDERSON .... Allan Hickle-Edwards
YOU .... Leslie Ball

Live music for the production was composed and performed by Jeffrey Willkomm and Bradley Gilbo.

An earlier draft of the play was presented by the Los Angeles Theatre Center in the spring of 1987.

ACKNOWLEDGEMENTS

The playwright wishes to thank the following individuals and organizations who contributed to the creation of *Foolin' Around With Infinity:*

Steven E. Alter
Berkeley Repertory Theatre
City Theatre Company, Pittsburgh
David Erickson
Deb Erickson
Mame Hunt
Los Angeles Theatre Center
Patty Lynch
Ruth Maleczech
The Minneapolis Office of Civil Defense
New York Stage and Film
Jane Norman
Bruce Odland
The Playwrights' Center, Minneapolis
Gayle Ritchie
George C. White
The cast of SURVIVE

CHARACTERS

YOU.................................. woman, any age.
MR. ANDERSON.................... man, any age.
LUKE ....Mac's daughter, 20's.
JOHN "JESSE" RANDALL....... the deputy, 20's.
ARTHUR "MAC" McCORMICK
...........................the crew commander, 50's.

TIME: The present, and elsewhere.

ACT I

SCENE: Two distinct environments.

At stage level is an open area which serves as the Fallout Shelter. Crude, bare walls and floor. Sparse.

On a raised platform is the Command Post of an underground missile silo. Bright, stark lighting. The room contains two consoles, twelve feet apart, with chairs behind them. Each console contains a computer, electronic coding devices, and a bank of flashing LIGHTS. Upstage, facing the audience, is a small red safe. Between the two consoles is a Monopoly game.

At extreme down right is a comfortable and fashionable chair with a small table and lamp nearby. On the table is a speaker phone and a glass of white wine.

At extreme down left is a chair which is identical to the audience seats. In front of it is a microphone.

Finally, a huge black and yellow "Fallout Shelter" insignia covers the upstage wall.

NOTE: Simplicity and velocity. The lines are the thought process.

(YOU enter through the audience. An USHER shows YOU to your seat – the down left chair. The USHER gives YOU a program. YOU sit.
A STAGEHAND enters and adjusts the microphone in front of YOU.
The house LIGHTS flicker, twice.
YOU speak into the microphone in front of YOU.)

YOU. YOU sit comfortably in the theatre.
YOU look around YOU.
YOU read from your program.

"Foolin' Around With Infinity. A Note from the Playwright.
"I had read about these guys. The keepers of the keys. Having a preoccupation with people of bizarre occupations, I did what I always do – I started a file. The chain of command – from my President giving the order to deploy the nuclear arsenal, to the commander and his deputy in the silo who turn the keys – was so wonderfully cryptic and Byzantine to me. It had the secret code and handshake feeling of a child's game. It was men playing at war. The file began to fill up.

"Into this file went the comment of former Assistant Secretary of Defense Martin Halperin:

'The NATO doctrine is that we will fight with conventional forces until we are losing, then we will fight with tactical nuclear weapons until we are losing, and then we will blow up the world.'

"Also into this file went the words of the Pentagon's T.K. Jones regarding how to protect oneself from nuclear fallout: 'Dig a hole. Cover it with two doors. Pile three feet of dirt on top. It's the dirt that does it.'

"In the summer of '82 I began working on a collaborative theatre piece called *Survive*. I worked in a sort of 'dueling playwrights' style with another Minneapolis playwright, David Erickson. David invented a character based entirely on Law and Order. To counter him, I invented a character based on Free Will. Instinct. Zen in overdrive. This character became a young woman. I named her Luke. David and I sat at two typewriters across a kitchen table and proceeded to have a war of language. I remember thinking that our major artistic achievement was the execution of the most perfect cup of Mocha Java coffee I'd ever had. Beyond that, we were stuck. We decided that we needed a specific environment in which our characters could duel. I suggested a Fallout Shelter (I had a file on that, too), and after another magnificent cup of coffee, we lit out on a field trip."

(*A loud, fast BLACKOUT.*
MR ANDERSON rides across the stage on a white bicycle. HE is dressed all in white, as the Popsicle Man. A SPOTLIGHT follows him.)

MR. ANDERSON. Note: The play you are about to see contains poetry, profanity, infidelity and Monopoly. Nobody sings. Leave now or deal with it. (*MR. ANDERSON is gone.*)

(*DARKNESS.*)

YOU. Okay. A light comes up on YOU.

(*It does.*)

YOU. YOU are here. The play you are about to be takes place during four hours on a winter night. Within this night are many days and nights. A small shaft of light comes up on Luke in the Fallout Shelter. Luke is twenty. YOU see her.

LUKE. This is home. I live here and listen to the time walk by me. I can tell – from every creak and groan of the floorboards – what time it is, who is going where, and who is doing what. (*Brief pause.*) The time now is eight-oh-two. Roland Grant has dropped a dime on the tile floor of the elevator. Tails.

YOU. Lights come up on Mac and Jesse in the Command Post. YOU see them.

(*MAC and JESSE are attaching their combination locks to the small red safe. THEY also carry large black notebooks.*)

JESSE. So what?

MAC. You made us late again.

JESSE. Two minutes.

MAC. I'll have to put it in the report.

JESSE. So what?

MAC. Watch your ass, Jesse boy.

JESSE. You call your daughter?

MAC. Got no daughter.

JESSE. How long's she been missing now?

MAC. I got no daughter and her name's not Linda.

LUKE. Call me Luke. When I was born, my grandparents each suggest a name to my parents: Linda, Ursula, Katherine, Elaine. I decided on Luke. It's an acronym.

MAC. You look like shit.

JESSE. Shut up, Mac.

MAC. Out of uniform.

JESSE. You're kidding.

MAC. Third time this week.

JESSE. I'm so glad you keep track.

MAC. Not supposed to see the white of your t-shirt. You know that.

JESSE. Yes. I know that.

MAC. I'll have to put it in the report.

JESSE. Do that.

MAC. And where the hell is your tie?
JESSE. In the oven at home.
YOU. Mac and Jesse play Monopoly. Luke speaks to YOU.

(*As LUKE speaks SHE takes one necktie after another from out of a Quaker Oats box, ties them and wears them loosely around her neck. By the end of her speech, she is wearing about ten of them.*)

LUKE. I wear ties. I wear them out of choice, not fashion. Nuclear Emergency Crisis Kit to Insure Eternity. NECKTIE. It's an acronym. I wear ties to save the world. You can't join NECKTIE. There is not a pledge week. There is not a telethon. You can't sign up for it at the mall. NECKTIE joins you. At birth. NECKTIE is survival by *instinct*, not by law. It is the moment-to-moment doing of what must be done. It is taking matters into your own hands. The time has come to wonder about the people around you. Who is taking stock and who is asleep at the wheel. Next time you pass someone – anyone – wearing a tie, ask them what it means to them. If they say something like: "It's just a tie." – pity them, hand them a dollar and move on. But if they say something that shows choice instead of fashion, if they say something like: "This tie represents my own humble way of dealing with a universe in chaos and a political reality that puts the legacy of Mozart in the hands of devious thugs with murderous intentions. This tie is my attempt at tomorrow." If they say something like that, you'll know they're a part of NECKTIE.

JESSE. That's not my job.

MAC. Then whose is it?

LUKE. Somebody's got to insure eternity.

JESSE. Well, it isn't mine.

MAC. Gimme the rules.

JESSE. I said no.

MAC. You think I'm gonna take your word for it?

JESSE. You're gonna take the money I gave you and that's all you're gonna take.

MAC. It's five hundred SHORT.

JESSE. OKAY. THAT'S IT. I'M NOT GONNA BE BANKER ANYMORE.

LUKE. Power is insidious and logarithmic. Power is the One-Hundredth Monkey Theory. At some point in the life of an idea, it tips the scale from obscurity to familiarity, and can no longer be ignored. It begins to flourish. Its time has come.

MAC. (*Handing Jesse a tie.*) Here. Put this on.

LUKE. (*Like lightning.*) It may dawn on that man this morning – whyamIputtingonthistie? It may dawn on that man this morning – whyamIputtingonthistie? It may dawn on thatmanandthatmanandthatman this morning – whyamIwhyamIputtingonthistie? It may dawn on

him this morning that suddenly he is no longer
seeking power. He is now *wielding* it.

JESSE. (*Having tied the tie haphazardly.*)
How's that?

LUKE. His time has come. The One-
Hundredth tie has been tied. Seizing the moment,
he executes a perfect full-Windsor and steps into
the world.

MAC. Jes.

JESSE. What?

LUKE. An idea is an amoeba. Attack it and
you double it.

MAC. Jes.

JESSE. WHAT?

MAC. We have always had that rule.

JESSE. Yeah. Right.

MAC. For a year now. Think about it.

YOU. YOU think about it.

JESSE. Wrong.

MAC. Since we started working together.

JESSE. Wrong.

MAC. The banker keeps five hundred in the
middle at all times. AT ALL TIMES, Jes. In case
someone lands on Free Parking.

JESSE. It's a stupid rule.

MAC. It was Brady's rule.

JESSE. That figures.

MAC. Watch it, Jes. I revered that man.

JESSE. Save it, Mac.

MAC. Brady knew how to be a banker. The man had a *gift*. The man was *born* to be a Monopoly banker.

JESSE. I am not listening to you.

MAC. A rule's a rule. You agreed to it.

JESSE. I was under duress.

MAC. We're all under duress. Think about it.

YOU. YOU think about it.

MAC. Give the five hundred, Jes.

JESSE. It's a stupid rule.

MAC. Give the five.

JESSE. It's a bonehead game.

MAC. I know that. You think I was born Sunday? You think I don't know that? (*Pause.*) But what else is there to do?

(*Silence.*)

YOU. Jesse gives Mac the five hundred. Jesse plays the game. Mac and Luke turn and look at one another. YOU imagine they are inside their modest, two-bedroom, inner-city home. Luke is nine.

MAC. What are you doing down there, honey?

LUKE. I'm listening.

MAC. The game's on up here. Want to come up and watch with me?

LUKE. No, thanks. Daddy, tell me the story.

MAC. Did you call your piano teacher back?

LUKE. No.

MAC. She wanted you to call her back.

LUKE. I know.

MAC. Return your phone calls and don't return your gifts. That's the secret, Luke. I want you to know that.

LUKE. Daddy, tell me the story.

MAC. You left your room up here a mess.

LUKE. Mom never made me clean my room.

MAC. She thought every flaw was a phase.

LUKE. Daddy, c'mon. Tell me the story of Bob.

MAC. Plumbbob.

LUKE. Right. *Plumbbob.* Operation Plumbbob.

MAC. Why do you want to hear that story again?

LUKE. I like the way you tell it.

MAC. What about your room? I don't like you staying down in the basement. There's no light. You should move your things back upstairs.

LUKE. Please, Daddy. Tell the story.

(*Silence.*)

YOU. No one knows if he told it then or not. YOU decide.

JESSE. Your turn, Mac.

MAC. What'd you do?

JESSE. Community Chest.

MAC. Sounds like my ex.

LUKE. The time now is eight thirty-seven. Elaine McElroy has locked her keys inside her Ford Fairlane. She is kicking the fender.

JESSE. And where is your ex nowadays?

MAC. You know, this new rule may help me out. This new integrated crew thing. They're splitting up the two-woman crews. Gonna start mixin' it up. Gonna start puttin' some *couples* down in these silos.

JESSE. You've got a partner.

MAC. Might trade you in on a beauty.

JESSE. None of those women are going to let themselves be locked underground with you.

MAC. That's not what Rynager said.

JESSE. Bullshit.

MAC. He called me.

JESSE. When?

MAC. Today. When I was up top.

JESSE. Rynager's on vacation.

MAC. Called from New Zealand. Checkin' up on us.

JESSE. Didn't call me.

MAC. Think a guy can afford *two* calls from New Zealand? Shit, it's already yesterday down there.

JESSE. He called your room?

MAC. New Zealand, Jes. That's one place I always wanted to see. Christ, I wish there'd been a war there.

JESSE. What'd he say?

MAC. Said they might fix me up with a beauty. Think about it, Jes. A man, a woman, and a room full of missiles. Now, *that* would be a relationship.

JESSE. And what happens to me?

MAC. Rynager's not sure you're still a good soldier. Wonders whether you've forgotten your oath. C'mon, let's hear that oath again. Say it with me —

JESSE. Roll the dice.

MAC. Most teams don't make it a year, you know that? But we have, Jes. You and me. One year tonight. It's a goddamn Kodak moment.

JESSE. Don't fuck with me. Rynager did not call.

MAC. Guys lose control, you know that?

JESSE. Roll the dice.

MAC. That's why the average age is twenty-five.

JESSE. Roll the dice.

MAC. They are overcome by the room. Tend to chase their Jack Daniels with Liquid Drano. Light themselves on fire during *The Beverly Hillbillies*. It ain't pretty.

JESSE. The dice.

MAC. Brady didn't make it a year, you know that? William Brady. Thought me and him'd be partners till the bitter end. But no dice.

JESSE. Roll.

(*MAC rolls the dice.*)

YOU. There is a knock at the door. YOU hear it.

(*Three huge KNOCKS, amplified.*)

MAC. What the hell is that?
JESSE. It's the door.
MAC. The what?
JESSE. The door.
MAC. What do you mean the DOOR. There is no DOOR. We are a quarter mile under Utah. People do not knock on our DOOR.

(*Three huge KNOCKS, amplified.*)

JESSE. I'll get it.

(*JESSE does not move.*
NOTE: The convention of the "door" consists of MR. ANDERSON either walking through the walls of the Command Post, or being discovered with light in various parts of the Command Post. There is never an actual opening or closing of a door.)

MR. ANDERSON. (*Appears, dressed as a traveling salesman.*) A good evening to you both and I know what you're thinking: yet another door-to-door salesman, we had two last week we had two last week I gave them toffee and coffee we had two last week. And now here I am, yet another American smile and shoeshine entrepreneur pounding the weather and braving the pavement, puttin' in a day's work for a dollar's pay, but gentlemen let me just say this: what I have in this briefcase goes beyond cookies, goes beyond cosmetics and will actually transcend Tupperware. Gentlemen, today is your trump card. May I elaborate?

(*Silence. MAC and JESSE stare at him. HE moves into the room.*)

MR. ANDERSON. Thank you. Now. As I open this briefcase, please remove the contents.

(*HE opens the briefcase and looks at Mac. MAC reaches into the briefcase and pulls out another briefcase.*)

MR. ANDERSON. Now. This is commonly called the what?
MAC. Huh?
MR. ANDERSON. The what?
MAC. The briefcase?
MR. ANDERSON. The *football*. This football is made of leather, but it is not the type that Johnny Unitas used to throw during the days when Raymond Berry ran buttonhooks and America ran the world. This football is carried by four military aides — each representing a branch of the

armed forces – they follow our President (bless him God) wherever he goes. Inside the football is a series of code words. It is with these code words that the President orders the Pentagon to give up its toys.

JESSE. (*Returns to the game.*) You gonna move?

MAC. (*To Mr. Anderson.*) What are you doing?

JESSE. I'm playing the game. You gonna move?

MAC. (*To Mr. Anderson.*) What are you doing here?

JESSE. Come play. He'll go away.

MAC. Jes, how did he –

JESSE. Ignore him. He'll go away. You gonna move or not?

MAC. I can't.

JESSE. Get over it, Mac. You can move.

MAC. I didn't get doubles.

JESSE. So?

MAC. I'm in jail. I can't move unless I –

JESSE. You can buy your way out.

MAC. No. I like it here.

MR. ANDERSON. So, let's say the President is dashing across the White House lawn to hop in his helicopter. The bevy of reporters dutifully gathered there watche as the President's Chief-of-Staff whispers something in his ear. The President stops. It's been a bad morning. He's realized he's just another lame duck-and-cover

President trying to think of a snappy title for his memoirs. Spending his days listening to his advisors saying the same photo-opportunistic things, and spending his nights listening to Frank Sinatra sing the same old goddamn songs. He stands tall. He beckons to one of the four military aides who surround him. The aide representing the Air Force – a twenty-year-old Nebraska farm boy with pink cheeks and white hair – brings the football, which is handcuffed to his wrist, over to the President. As the reporters' pencils and microphones fall to the ground, the President – standing tall – directs the Pentagon to make war.

MAC. Jes, are you hearing this?

JESSE. You own Baltic?

MR. ANDERSON. The Pentagon sends the alert code to the underground missile silos. At each site are two men – men very much like you. One man is the commander. The other the deputy. They are the keepers of the keys.

JESSE. You own Baltic or not?

MAC. Yeah.

JESSE. Why'd you buy *Baltic?*

MAC. I landed on it.

JESSE. Rent's only four dollars.

MAC. So?

JESSE. So, it's a stupid purchase.

MAC. Not if I land on Mediterranean.

JESSE. Why would you buy *that?*

MAC. Sounds exotic.

JESSE. Sounds like a sofa.

MR. ANDERSON. These two men very much like you decode the incoming messages separately. Then compare them to make sure they match.

MAC. Jes, how'd this guy get in here?

MR. ANDERSON. If the codes match —

JESSE. What guy? He's gone. Play the game.

MR. ANDERSON. — They each open one of the two combinations locks to the little red safe.

YOU. Mr. Anderson shows YOU the little red safe.

MAC. I won a beauty contest. Pay up.

JESSE. You?

MAC. Pay up.

JESSE. That an order?

MAC. It's a rule.

JESSE. You've got rules where other men have skin.

MR. ANDERSON. The little red safe cannot be opened by one man alone for neither man has the combination to both locks.

MAC. GO AWAY.

JESSE. *What?*

MR. ANDERSON. The little red safe cannot be opened by one man alone for neither man has the combination to both locks.

MAC. GO AWAY.

JESSE. *He's gone.* Water Works. Roll the dice.

MAC. I know.

JESSE. You pay me ten times what you roll.

MAC. I know.

JESSE. I know you know.

MR. ANDERSON. The locks are issued secretly and each man brings his own lock down to the silo for each shift.

YOU. YOU watch Commander McCormick shake the dice in his right hand.

MAC. Talked to Delgado last weekend.

JESSE. There went your weekend.

MAC. He told me your combination.

(*Long silence.*)

YOU. Following the long silence, YOU watch Commander McCormick throw the dice.

MAC. (*Throws dice and smiles.*) What do you think of that, Jes?

MR. ANDERSON. Once the safe is opened and the sealed authenticator inside matches the incoming message, the two men very much like you take out separate firing keys.

JESSE. (*Suddenly, to Mr. Anderson.*) GET OUT OF HERE.

MAC. He's gone.

MR. ANDERSON. The men each carry their firing keys to consoles which are about twelve feet apart.

YOU. Mr. Anderson shows you the consoles.

JESSE. How'd you get my combo?

MAC. 'Member eight months ago when Delgado went down to work his shift and his lock was jammed? He had to borrow one and no one would lend him one but *you*.

MR. ANDERSON. The men insert their firing keys into the consoles.

JESSE. I swore Delgado to secrecy.

MAC. I did you one better.

MR. ANDERSON. The men turn the keys simultaneously.

MAC. I took him drinking.

MR. ANDERSON. MoscowIwasn'tkidding-Pow.

MAC. You're a rare breed, Jes.

MR. ANDERSON. TeheranIwasn'tkidding-Pow.

MAC. And I love you for that.

JESSE. You're a criminal, Mac.

MR. ANDERSON. BeirutIwasn'tkidding-Pow.

JESSE. You're both fucking criminals —

MAC. What's the harm?

MR. ANDERSON. ManaguaIwasn'tkidding-Pow.

JESSE. You could open the safe on your *own*.

MR. ANDERSON. SantiagoIwasn'tkidding-Pow.

MAC. And where would you be?

MR. ANDERSON. HavanaIwasn'tkidding-Pow.

JESSE. Shot and lying in the corner.

MR. ANDERSON. MontgomeryIwasn't-
kiddingPow.

MAC. Would I do that?

JESSE. You'd write a How-To book.

MR. ANDERSON. (*Name of your city*)
Iwasn'tkiddingPow.

MAC. I still couldn't turn both keys. *Think
about it.*

YOU. YOU do.

JESSE. It's all I think about.

MR. ANDERSON. Silence.

(*Silence.*)

YOU. YOU hear the silence.

MR. ANDERSON. And finally, gentlemen —

JESSE. MAC, GET HIM OUT OF HERE.

MR. ANDERSON. The most wise and
wonderful thing about the system is this:

MAC. You should acquire social graces, Jes.

MR. ANDERSON. If, at *any time* while
working together in the Command Post one of
these men suspects his partner of sabotage —

MAC. You should tell him to have a nice day.

MR. ANDERSON. — He has orders to shoot
and kill his partner on the spot.

(*Silence.*)

YOU. YOU see Mac and Jesse look at each other. YOU see their eyes meet the way men's eyes do. Several feet in front of their faces.

MR. ANDERSON. Thank you so much for your time.

MAC. I'll see you out.

(*MAC does not move. MR. ANDERSON is gone.*)

MAC. Christ, it's nice to have company for a change.

JESSE. You know, over this past year, everything living in your brain has gradually moved out.

MAC. I'd like four houses, please.

JESSE. What?

MAC. Four houses. I want to buy four houses.

JESSE. You don't have a monopoly.

MAC. Sure I do.

JESSE. On what?

MAC. I own all four railroads.

JESSE. You want to put houses on your railroads?

MAC. Relax. I'll build bridges.

LUKE. The sign had never caught my eye. For years I'd walked across the bridge and through the alley and past this building. For years I'd seen the railroad ties, the have-and-have-nots, the whitewashed windows and pigeonlittered cement. But the sign had never caught my eye.

I am walking now with a suitcase in my hand. He has frightened me again and it is time to relocate to a new basement. I am walking across the bridge and through the alley and past this building. I am walking and I am thinking. The mind is a manic juggler. I am thinking simultaneously about red M&M's, nuclear winter, the Lincoln memorial, and the hole in my left sock. I want to find things I've lost. I want to jump more. When I was a kid I always jumped a couple times a day. I jumped because jumping was something I didn't need a ticket to. I jumped because I had not yet given in to gravity. I jumped because as a kid I was immortal.

There, on the wall above the shattered door, was the sign that had never caught my eye. It hovered like a footnote and beckoned like the Popsicle Man.

"Fallout Shelter."

As I step inside and close the door behind me, I am thinking simultaneously about Dylan Thomas, nuclear winter, the cost of a perm, and my fear of turning into a McPerson.

YOU. YOU imagine Luke, several years later, living in her conservative townhouse community. Luke is thirty-three.

(*LUKE sits in the down right chair. Talks into her speaker phone. Sips her wine.*)

MAC. Are you there, honey?

LUKE. Yes, Daddy.

MAC. The connection's bad. Can you hear me?

LUKE. Daddy, I really can't talk right now.

MAC. Honey, I just called to let —

LUKE. Just a sec, Daddy. Can you hold? (*SHE presses a button on the phone. SHE turns to the audience.*) My radicalism was a phase. And, like any phase, it had motion. I became disenchanted. I became a loner. I became a wind-chime artist. I became a mystic. I became an expert. I became an author. I became a lecturer. I became a cult figure. I became a media darling. I became a commodity. I became a corporation, a conservative, a conundrum and a condo-babe. And the point is this: I do not think of *this* as a phase. This is a calling. (*Presses button on the phone.*) Hi, Daddy. Thanks for holding. What's up?

MAC. Honey, are you coming by on Sunday?

LUKE. Daddy, I really can't. There's a white sale. I can't pass it up. Gregory and I will stop by next week, I promise. Are the nurses treating you well?

MAC. Come Sunday.

LUKE. Did you get the truffles I sent?

MAC. Come Sunday.

LUKE. I don't want you to fill your mind for one minute with thoughts of the exorbitant costs which Gregory and I are dealing with just to keep you in bed and medicated.

MAC. Come Sunday.

LUKE. Bye, Daddy. Always take your morning walk and your afternoon nap. That's the secret. I want you to know that.

MAC. Please, honey.

LUKE. The fresh air is an elixir.

MAC. Please come.

LUKE. Ciao. (*Leaves the downright chair.*)

JESSE. Mac, when do you suppose we'll die?

MAC. Ciao.

JESSE. Right. Ciao. Adios. When do you think that will be?

LUKE. The time now is nine eleven. Nancy Wood has finally found her contact lens on the low F-sharp of her piano.

MAC. Well ...

LUKE. Now she's lost her music.

MAC. I'd say we'll die either the moment before we turn the keys, or six weeks later when the supplies run out.

(*Silence.*)

JESSE. There are no supplies down here.

MAC. It's an oversight. They'll get to it.

(*Silence.*)

JESSE. What would we do for those six weeks?

MAC. Same thing we've been doing for a year.

(*Silence.*)

JESSE. You got any other games at home?

MAC. Scrabble.

JESSE. Bring that.

MAC. I hate Scrabble.

JESSE. It'll keep you sane.

MAC. If I wanted to be sane, I'd get a transfer. 'Sides, Scrabble's hard. I always get the J's and X's.

JESSE. It's just spelling.

MAC. I don't spell so good.

JESSE. You what?

MAC. I was absent that day.

JESSE. Oh, great.

MAC. Roll the dice.

JESSE. That's great.

MAC. The D-I-C-E. ROLL THEM.

JESSE. A code comes in here, you misspell the word, you transmit it wrong – and we blow up Salt Lake City.

MAC. I'd be a hero.

YOU. YOU imagine Mac is making a bologna sandwich for his sixteen-year-old daughter as the Jetsons are heard in black-and-white from another room.

MAC. Go.

LUKE. Too much mustard.

MAC. Better?

LUKE. Yeah.

MAC. Go.

LUKE. We got tomato?

MAC. No.

LUKE. Oh.

MAC. Go.

LUKE. Are you the man who hit one of the most dramatic home runs in baseball history?

MAC. No, I am not Bobby Thompson. Go.

LUKE. Are you the singer who was married on the *Tonight Show?*

MAC. No, I am not Tiny Tim. Go.

LUKE. Damn.

MAC. What?

LUKE. We got Swiss cheese?

MAC. You want to pay for *holes?* We got American cheese. Go.

LUKE. Are you a famous poet who died a tragic death at age thirty-nine?

MAC. No, I am not ... uh ... I am not — Conway Twitty.

LUKE. Wrong.

MAC. Who?

LUKE. Dylan Thomas.

MAC. WHO?

LUKE. He wrote. He died. Trust me.

MAC. Direct question. Go.

LUKE. We got lettuce?

MAC. No. Go.

LUKE. Are you a person who achieved fame mainly through the sciences?

MAC. Yes.

LUKE. Were you a member of the Manhattan Project?

MAC. Damn.

LUKE. Were you?

MAC. Yes.

JESSE. Mac?

MAC. Yes?

JESSE. You ever written anything at all?

MAC. No.

JESSE. Ever?

MAC. No.

LUKE. Were you the father of Project Panda?

MAC. Yes.

JESSE. Grocery lists, Christmas cards, nothing?

MAC. No.

JESSE. Everyone writes something, Mac.

MAC. Jes, I write reports every night and when our shift is over I burn them — according to regulations — so no one will ever know they existed.

LUKE. Did you nickname the first hydrogen bomb "Mike?"

MAC. Yes.

JESSE. I'm writing a book.

MAC. Oh, good.

JESSE. And you're in it.

MAC. Oh, good.

LUKE. Did you detonate "Mike" on the island of Elugelab?

MAC. Yes.

JESSE. Want to know what I'm writing?

MAC. No.

LUKE. Did the entire island turn to vapor and vanish forever?

MAC. Yes.

LUKE. Did you wire the boys at Los Alamos and tell them: "IT'S A BOY!?"

MAC. Yes.

JESSE. Want to know what I'm saying about you?

MAC. No.

LUKE. Did you state that "If you explode all the nuclear weapons in all the arsenals of the world a large fraction of humanity will not be injured, and the damage will be more or less confined to the places where the hostilities occurred?"

MAC. YES.

LUKE. And are you credited with inspiring the "Star Wars" defense system?

MAC. YES.

LUKE. You are Edward Teller.

MAC. Damnit, Luke. How do you *do* that?

LUKE. (*Moving away.*) I know what you like.

JESSE. I'm writing my autobiography.

MAC. Sounds like something you read in a car.

JESSE. It's a book so people know who I was.

MAC. Who's gonna care? You got a Certs?

JESSE. How do you want people to remember you?

MAC. I'd be happy with my face on a stamp. Check your pockets.

JESSE. You have no idea what we are paid to do here.

MAC. We are paid to shut up and do our job. You got a Certs or not?

JESSE. And if we ever actually *do* our job, we will *have* no job.

MAC. No Certs, huh?

JESSE. We will have no nothing.

MAC. *Lifesaver?*

JESSE. Jesus, Mac – what about your family? Your daughter?

MAC. I got no daughter and her name's not Linda. Got no family. Got no loved ones. Got no outstanding bills. I got his job and I love it here and you should love it, too. We are *pioneers*, Jes. We are standing on the precipice of the human experiment. And when pioneers confront new territory, some must become legends and some must get killed. This, Jesse, is our situation. And our situation is our legacy.

JESSE. I can only hope your mouth doesn't connect to your mind.

MAC. And another thing – I *never* read a book they haven't made into a movie.

LUKE, YOU WANT TO GO TO A MOVIE? LUKE, I KNOW YOU'RE DOWN THERE. DAMNIT, I AM YOUR FATHER AND YOU CAN'T RUN FROM ME AND YOU CAN'T STAY IN THE BASEMENT FOREVER.

YOU. Luke tells YOU a story.

LUKE. My father.

My father took home movies. Bad home movies – although that phrase may be redundant. These were the early days of the home movie phenomenon, when the cameras were square and bulky and had brown imitation leather casings. My father used his camera every Christmas to take action shots of Mom and I doing our yearly film ritual. This consisted of standing in front of our silver aluminum Christmas tree, waving, holding new articles of clothing up to our bodies, smiling, waving, pointing to the red and green decorative balloons, still more waving. And each year, propped up against the base of the tree, there was an empty shirt box. On the back of this box my father had written the year in black marker. Mom and I stood there, an advertisement for a year gone by. Preserved in living color. Sort of.

My father's camera produced home movies that were dark. Very dark. The Christmas shots looked like two sets of teeth hovering near an unidentified silver object. My father turned on more lights in the room each year. He brought in lamps from other rooms. One year we even set the tree up in the kitchen – it being the best lit room. No luck. Dark. Very dark. It never dawned on my father to A: have the camera repaired; B: buy a new camera; or C: take the movies on Christmas morning when the room was engulfed in sunlight. My father is not just set in his ways. He is buried in them.

After years of bad home movies, my father had a plan. Several weeks prior to Christmas he holed up in the basement and began to construct what he called THE DEVICE. THE DEVICE was a sort of wooden cross built of two-by-fours, with a metal handle attached to the back. This wooden structure was fitted with sockets, and wired to house eight 200-watt directional light bulbs. The huge black cord which ran to the wall outlet was 15 feet long – to allow for maximum maneuverability, he said.

My father motioned Mom and I to stand in front of the tree. The shirt box was already inscribed and in place. He grabbed the handle of THE DEVICE and with the other hand plugged it in.

The light was blinding. The room was transfixed. Several balloons popped. Sparks flew from the outlet. My father held THE DEVICE in one hand – five feet from our faces – and with his free hand he grabbed his camera. Purely out of habit, I suppose, Mom and I began our little film ritual. But we were dazed with wattage. Squinting. Tilting our heads. Lifting gifts in front of our eyes as shields. Obviously in pain as we waved to the best of our ability. I could not see my father's reaction to this experiment, but a moment later both THE DEVICE and the camera went crashing to the ground.

After Mom and I had rubbed the spots from our eyes, we glanced up. My father was gone. Mom put on rubber gloves and unplugged THE DEVICE. I walked over to the camera which lay on the carpet. It had jammed in the "ON" position when it fell, so it continued to record the event. I had the film developed and watched it in secret.

It is vibrant. There are two women, young and old, penetrated by light. White hot faces. Glowing to the bone. There is sudden motion. Floorwallceiling. Floorwallceiling. Then stillness. The camera is focused on a white hot corner of the ceiling. Suspended in this corner is a small, green balloon. This shot holds for seven minutes. Then, sudden blackness.

MAC. C'mon, honey. It's a triple feature at the Drive-In.

LUKE. I once tried to show this film to my father.

MAC. You can sit on my lap and steer.

LUKE. He told me to clean my room.

MAC. We'll bring your pj's and a grocery bag of popcorn.

LUKE. And he never took another home movie.

MAC. Luke, your mom would want you to go.

YOU. YOU watch Luke think about her mom. (*Pause.*) Luke tells YOU another story.

LUKE. My mom.

My mom wanted a new life. She went out and got one. The new life got old.

YOU. Luke finishes the story for YOU.

LUKE. She moved to Indiana. She wears blue pumps on the Avenue.

MAC. Come on upstairs, honey. Please?

(*Three huge KNOCKS, amplified.*)

JESSE. I'll get it. (*JESSE does not move.*)

MR. ANDERSON. (*Appears, wearing a bright orange jumpsuit and hat.*) Thanks for calling Mr. Anderson's Walk-A-Pet. Designed for those urban dwellers who simply don't have time to get that pooch or pussycat out of the house and into the world. Mr. Anderson's Walk-A-Pet service includes free waste pickup and a full pet massage for those soon-to-be-tired little paws. Any questions?

MAC. What the hell's happened to security around here?

MR. ANDERSON. Safe and secure from the moment we step out your door because Mr. Anderson's Walk-A-Pet service has a pet control device to suit every pet and every situation.

MAC. Jes, say something.

JESSE. Ignore him. He'll go away.

MR. ANDERSON. (*Producing a small cloth leash.*) For the polite little puppy. (*Producing a typical leather leash.*) For the lifelong companion. (*Producing a heavy leather leash with studs.*) For the adventuresome animal of distinction. (*Producing a pair of handcuffs.*) For the devious dog of knowledge. (*Producing a miniature straitjacket.*) For the ferocious Cro-Magnon mutt. (*Producing a large handgun.*) For man's best friend. Mr. Anderson's Walk-A-Pet will KEEP YOUR DOG IN LINE. Any questions?

MAC. I. Have. No Pets.

MR. ANDERSON. This system works for children as well.

MAC. I. Have. No. Children.

MR. ANDERSON. You're lying. I don't know you well enough to tell *why* you're lying. But you're lying. (*To Jesse.*) He's lying. (*To Mac.*) Is she dead or missing?

MAC. WHO?

MR. ANDERSON. Your daughter.

LUKE. Daddy!

MAC. That's not the Popsicle Man, honey.

MR. ANDERSON. God-given name of Linda.

LUKE. Daddy, I heard the bell!

MAC. That was not the Popsicle Man.

JESSE. Claims he's got no family at all.

MAC. The Popsicle Man doesn't come by here anymore.

MR. ANDERSON. Is she dead or missing?

MAC. I. Do.

MR. ANDERSON. Is she hiding?

MAC. Not.

MR. ANDERSON. Is she lost?

MAC. Hear. You.

MR. ANDERSON. Is she living in a Fallout Shelter thinking simultaneously about "The Brady Bunch," nuclear winter, tarot cards and the N.R.A.?

MAC. (*Suddenly, to Mr. Anderson.*) "Sufficient shelter is available for the entire population if properly distributed."

JESSE. Mac, that's bullshit and you know it.

MAC. (*More rapidly, to Jesse.*) "Sufficient shelter is available for the entire population if properly distributed."

JESSE. (*Overlapping.*) This is not like hiding from a hurricane.

MAC. Those shelters are built to withstand an overhead blast of –

JESSE. Mac, you know those shelters are gonna shatter like glass.

MAC. IT'S AN OVERSIGHT.

MR. ANDERSON. I sincerely hope you find her.

MAC. THEY'LL GET TO IT.

MR. ANDERSON. (*To audience.*) For your information, the nearest shelter to this theatre is at (*give address or name of nearest shelter*).

MAC. You can go now. We're not interested.

MR. ANDERSON. Then please keep this litter bag with our compliments. Good day.

(*MR. ANDERSON gives MAC the bag and is gone.*)

LUKE. The time now is nine fifty-seven. Cathy Erskine wonders why the fruit in the bowl has gone rotten.

JESSE. (*Leans in close to Mac, very sincere.*) Hey, Mac. You really got a daughter? You can tell me. I'd like to know.

MAC. (*Leans in close to Jesse, very sincere.*) Well, Jes. I'll tell you.

YOU. YOU imagine a scene in soft, yet masculine light, where the two men ramble eloquently through stories about their families, their hopes, their dreams, their fears. (*Silence.*) It does not happen.

MAC. (*Leaning back.*) That guy reminds me of how Brady died.

JESSE. What, the gun?

MAC. No. The leash.

JESSE. What?

LUKE. (*From the downright chrome chair.*) We really need to be going, Daddy. Gregory has a meeting and I have a facial.

MAC. William Brady. Best partner I ever had. Ugliest man born this century. Died a virgin at forty-nine. I used to call him Unmarked Bill.

JESSE. Died how?

LUKE. We all know the story, Daddy. Why don't you take your nap?

MAC. Well, Jes. I'll tell you. William Brady was walking in the field by his farmhouse. He caught sight of a timber wolf starin' him square in the eyes. About five feet away. Growling at that

man like no woman ever had. This wolf was
mean as a grizzly and twice as hungry. This wolf
was dealing with the issues that are in capital
letters. This wolf was determined to make an
amendment to the food chain. William Brady, the
best partner I ever had, did not panic. Instead, he
remembered a story about what a proud fighting
animal the wolf is, and that if a predator offers his
neck in surrender to the wolf ... the wolf will not
harm him. So William Brady undid the top two
buttons of his shirt, tilted his head, and offered his
neck to that wolf. And he'd be here today were it
not for his eyesight.

LUKE. Really?

JESSE. What do you mean?

MAC. Wasn't a wolf. It was a Doberman.
Rabid as the night is long. Went for that neck like
a boy to a cheerleader. Bill wasn't unmarked for
long.

LUKE. That's quite a story, Daddy.

MAC. He was quite a guy.

LUKE. We'll see you next week. (*Leaves the
down right chair.*)

MAC. Loved him like a brother-in-law.

JESSE. Tell that story a lot, Mac?

MAC. Every bar in this state.

JESSE. Ever told anyone the truth?

MAC. 'Bout what?

JESSE. How Brady died.

MAC. I just told you.

LUKE. You know how, as a kid, you always wanted to go visit your Dad at work? Sit at Dad's desk. Wear Dad's hat. Meet Dad's boss. It is amazing to me that his man came home night after night and I jumped in his lap – and I had no idea where he had been.

JESSE. I'd wager it wasn't a Doberman killed Brady.

MAC. You got. No. Proof.

LUKE. A year ago I finally found out.

(A loud, fast BLACKOUT. YOU remain lit.)

YOU. YOU imagine an intermission. YOU rise from your chair and begin the pleasantries and pirouettes of the social event. A Coke is purchased. A candy is unwrapped. There is an ocean of ashtrays and a dearth of bathrooms. Leaning against a wall which you hope is structural, but suspect is decorative, YOU glance again at your program.

"David and I arrived at the Minneapolis Office of Civil Defense, recently placed under the jurisdiction of the Federal Emergency Management Agency (*FEMA*) by the Reagan administration. The building was an old firehouse which had been converted to offices. It was filled with old furniture and new brochures."

(*MR. ANDERSON enters and stands near YOU. HE waves, shyly. MR. ANDERSON wears slacks, an old cardigan sweater, glasses, small bow tie, a construction helmet that bears a Fallout Shelter insignia, and HE carries a clipboard and a styrofoam cup of coffee.*)

YOU. "A man greeted us. He wore glasses and an old cardigan sweater and looked like my Uncle Al. He was the only employee in sight, and he was thrilled to talk to us. It was clear that having people come to his office interested in Civil Defense was a new and exciting experience for him. This was, after all, the "if-it-happens-it-happens-80's" and not the "prepare-for-the-worst-50's.""

(*MR. ANDERSON shakes your hand.*)

YOU. He shook our hands. He gave us Maxwell House in styrofoam cups. He gave us very specific information on safety procedures during floods, hurricanes and tornadoes. I asked about protection from nuclear fallout. His hand tightened around his styrofoam cup."

MR. ANDERSON. "We're a lot more prepared for a tornado, *that* I can tell you."

YOU. "Are the shelters safe? Are they stocked with supplies?"

MR. ANDERSON. "Follow me."

YOU. "—He said, leading us into the basement of the building. Above a doorway was the familiar black and yellow Fallout Shelter insignia. The room was like a concrete shoebox. Dark and damp. Against one wall was a huge stack of boxes."

MR. ANDERSON. "Those boxes there. Those're your supplies. Food, water, first aid, radiation detection kits, other stuff. You could go a couple weeks down here if you had to."

YOU. "I was impressed. I mentioned that it looked like an awful lot of boxes to contain only two weeks of supplies. He pulled two of the boxes away from the rest."

MR. ANDERSON. "These belong down here. The others are for the rest of the city."

YOU. "Pardon me?"

MR. ANDERSON. "They've been here since '71. We just never got 'em distributed. That's why there's so many here."

YOU. "So, all the other shelters are empty?" (*Pause.*) He nodded.

(*HOUSE LIGHTS flicker, twice. MR. ANDERSON turns and leaves.*)

YOU. A light flickers, interrupting YOU. YOU close your program. YOU navigate the path back to your seat. Finishing your Coke, YOU toss the empty cup toward a trash can from a distance of four feet. A voice behind YOU murmurs "Nice shot." YOU walk a little taller. Your seat is as YOU left it. The intermission ends.

(*LIGHTS come up on the Command Post.*)

YOU. YOU see the Command Post. YOU see Mac and Luke there.

(*MAC and LUKE stand in the Command Post with their backs to the audience. LUKE wears a military uniform that is much too big for her. SHE also wears a very obviously fake mustache. JESSE is gone.*)

MAC. Follow me.

(*THEY turn in unison and move into the room.*)

MAC. Sit there.

(*LUKE sits in Jesse's chair. MAC sits in his own. Silence. LUKE removes her hat.*)

MAC. Leave that on. We've got to be certain.
LUKE. (*The clothes.*) Who does this stuff belong to?
MAC. Brady.
LUKE. Your boss?
MAC. My partner. Ex-partner.

(*LUKE starts to touch a dial on the console.*)

MAC. Don't touch that, honey.

LUKE. Why?

MAC. Only Daddy can touch that.

LUKE. I'm not a kid anymore, you know.

MAC. I know that.

LUKE. So?

MAC. So?

LUKE. So, are you going to answer my question?

MAC. It's a silly question, honey.

LUKE. Don't call me honey, okay? Well?

(*Silence.*)

MAC. No.

LUKE. No, you won't answer it?

MAC. No, I don't think a Boston fern could live down here.

LUKE. English Ivy?

MAC. I don't think so.

LUKE. Philodendron could.

MAC. There's no light.

LUKE. There's no light at home and they live there.

MAC. Things need light.

LUKE. There's no light at home and we live there.

(*Silence.*)

MAC. It's okay now.

LUKE. (*Takes off her hat and mustache.*) Gum, Daddy?

MAC. Do I want some?

LUKE. Do you have some?

MAC. Oh ... yeah. (*Gives her the gum.*)

(*Silence.*)

MAC. You want to play Monopoly?

LUKE. Is that what you do here?

MAC. Sure. C'mon.

LUKE. I don't want to.

MAC. How 'bout a round of Botticelli? You pick the name. Go.

LUKE. No.

MAC. Ping pong?

LUKE. Huh-uh.

MAC. Pac Man?

LUKE. You got Pac Man?

MAC. These little screens have everything. You name a country and we'll gobble it up.

LUKE. No, thanks.

MAC. Then what do you want to do? You want a Coke?

LUKE. No.

MAC. You want to go for a ride?

LUKE. Tell me the story of Plumbbob. Operation Plumbbob.

MAC. Luke, c'mon —

LUKE. "On a lovely day in June, 1957, there was a young army soldier stationed in Nevada. This soldier —"

MAC. Look, the board is all set up. You can use Brady's money and property. He's got both utilities. It'll be really fun. He won't mind.

LUKE. Where is he tonight?

MAC. Mittendorf and Sons.

LUKE. That a hospital?

MAC. Close.

YOU. YOU see them look at each other. YOU see them try to visualize the other as young and small and innocent. The father is remembering. The daughter is imagining.

LUKE. Why won't you tell me the story?

(*MAC is silent. LUKE moves away.*)

LUKE. Tell me what these mean, Daddy. Inhibit. Hold. No-Go. Security Fault. Warhead Alarm.

MAC. Every few seconds each missile is electronically interrogated.

LUKE. Like a pop quiz.

MAC. It's really something, honey. I'd get you one for Christmas if I could. Say you hear a little "bleep" or see one of these panels light up. It means there's been a slight malfunction in the system that controls the missile.

LUKE. And you put on gloves and go fix it.

MAC. No. You just dial that particular missile and get a printout. Then you enter that information back into the system and the fault is corrected automatically. It's really something, don't you think?

(*Silence.*)

LUKE. Mom used to tell me you were a dry cleaner.
MAC. Did you believe her?
LUKE. No. Didn't believe barber or chimney sweep either.

(*Silence.*)

MAC. So, what do you think now that you know?
LUKE. I think I'd drink scotch, too.

(*Silence.*)

MAC. I care for you, honey.
LUKE. My name's Luke.

(*Three huge KNOCKS, amplified.*)

LUKE. I'll get it.
MAC. Don't move.
LUKE. Huh?
MAC. I said don't move.

LUKE. Daddy, someone's at the –
MAC. Luke, there is. No. Door.

(*Three huge KNOCKS, amplified.*)

LUKE. You're not gonna get that?
MAC. No.
LUKE. Might be the Popsicle Man.
MAC. No.
LUKE. Might be Mom.
MAC. Luke we do not have an address. We do not have a street. We are not even on the goddamn map. I don't care if it's *Halloween*, people can't just –

(*Three huge KNOCKS, amplified.*)

MAC. There are guys assigned to this base who work here their whole lives and DIE without ever seeing –

(*Three huge KNOCKS, amplified.*)

MAC. We are supposed to be INVISIBLE.

(*Three huge KNOCKS, amplified.*)

LUKE. I'm getting the door now.

(*LUKE does not move. MR. ANDERSON appears,
wearing a long hippie robe, beads, a long wig,
and carrying a newspaper.*)

MR. ANDERSON. Hey, cat. Hey, big guy.
Hell of a door. Hell of a place. Hell of a way to
spend a Sunday, huh?

MAC. Who are you?

MR. ANDERSON. I am as I appear. Neo-
liberal E.R.A. pro-choice save the whales ban
handguns bread not bombs but I can change my
mind and I can turn on a dime and what would
you like me to be?

MAC. What do you want here?

MR. ANDERSON. I want to look at the two
bedroom.

MAC. *What?*

MR. ANDERSON. Did you rent it? I bet you
rented it? I got up and I said Mr. Anderson get
over there, get over there, Mr. Anderson, cause
that place is gonna rent is gonna move is gonna
go is gonna be gobbled up like 'shrooms at a Dead
concert.

LUKE. It hasn't been rented.

MR. ANDERSON. Thank God. And garden
level, too. Does it have a shower? Can I put one in?
Can I have a cat? Do you have a cat? Do you have a
drinking problem?

MAC. Let me explain something.

MR. ANDERSON. I know when I'm about to
hear the word LEASE and let me say that a LEASE

does not frighten me. I can ride the river, I can go the distance with a LEASE, big guy.

MAC. Let me explain something.

MR. ANDERSON. I don't have parties. I don't have a stereo. I don't snore. I don't smoke. I go outside to talk. People won't come over. I won't come over. I'll stay with friends. You won't know I'm here. Do I pay heat?

MAC. Let me explain something.

MR. ANDERSON. You won't mind a couple holes in the wall, right? You won't mind if I change the curtains and rewire this room and knock out that wall and put in a fireplace and build a deck and convert to solar and become a waterbed showroom? I've got references.

MAC. Let me *kill you.*

MR. ANDERSON. Walk soft, cat. Walk slow, big guy. (*Pulls off the hippie robe. revealing a dapper, conservative three-piece suit. HE removes the wig, as well.*) I am as I appear. Ultra-conservative N.R.A. feed Jane Fonda to the whales pro-life burn Huck Finn prayer in the schools and a strong defense but I can change my mind and I can turn on a dime and what would you like me to be?

YOU. Mac begins to comb his hair with a small, yellow comb. YOU watch him.

MAC. (*Turning from Mr. Anderson, addressing the audience.*) I live here. I live on the earth above here. I walk around on Utah. I breathe air that once was sea.

Every night I turn off Conway Twitty and I leave my single room up top. I walk down the hall past the kitchen that smells of garlic and the other single rooms that smell of Old Spice. I press a button. I step through a door. And I ride a bullet into the earth. Every God. Damn. Night.

I work my shift. (*He pulls some hairs out of the yellow comb.*) And little pieces of my head keep falling out. (*He watches the hairs waft to the ground in front of him.*)

Four hours later I press a button, step through the door, and ride that bullet up top like a missile. I go to my single room. And I put another bookmark in the Bible.

(*Silence.*)

YOU. YOU watch Mr. Anderson leave. He does not have an exit line.

LUKE. Daddy.

MAC. Yes?

LUKE. Do you know where the missiles are going to go?

MAC. No. I don't ask.

LUKE. Did you ask Mom where she was going to go?

(*Silence.*)

MAC. You want a Coke?

LUKE. No.

MAC. You want to go for a ride?

LUKE. No.

MAC. C'mon, gimme a break. Every kid ALWAYS wants one of those things. A COKE OR A RIDE. C'MON. PICK ONE.

LUKE. No.

MAC. You want to go home, then?

LUKE. No, Daddy. I'm not going home, anymore.

MAC. What the hell are you —

LUKE. You scare me, Daddy. Some nights I sneak upstairs and watch you sleep. I eat pretzels at the foot of your bed. I watch your hairs crawl out of your head and lie on your pillow. When you sleep, you look dead.

MAC. Don't run, Luke. There's nowhere to run.

LUKE. Bye, Dad. I left a note for you in the basement. (*Leaves.*)

YOU. YOU see Luke leave. YOU see Mac begin to comb his hair.

JESSE. (*Steps into an area of LIGHT downstage and speaks to the audience.*) I used to live in an old house in a college town. I had nine roommates. We did what the times told us to do. We ate mushrooms and wore bandanas and wrote FUCK on things that were not moving. We drank tequila and beer and drove around with Lou Reed to sober up. I am not proud of those days, but they reside in me. They are the days I first bordered on realism. They are the days I first flirted with

maturity. And avarice. And cowardice. And
helplessness.

(*JESSE moves to his seat in the Command Post.
The only light is a shaft of LIGHT on him.
The rest of the Command Post, including
MAC at his chair, is in darkness.*)

JESSE. Eight of us are crammed into a 1961
Rambler. We are coming home from a concert.
My ninth roommate, Henry, has stayed at home.
My friend Connie is driving. Three in front.
Five in back. We have done a lot of mushrooms
and smoked a lot of dope. The Moody Blues spew
pop philosophy through the tiny in-dash radio. We
are eight bodies in a metal box moving seventy
miles an hour. And, as always at this point in the
evening, the conversation consists of talking
about *just how stoned we are.* We are laughing
riotously at our lack of motor skills. And upon
experiencing any new visual sensation – a
billboard, a bumper *sticker*, a windshield *wiper* –
we scream in joy at the top of our lungs. It was at
this moment that Connie – with both hands still
propped up on the wheel – very softly said: "God,
this is good shit. I'm so glad I'm not driving."
    The rest of us froze. Connie, with both hands
still propped up on the wheel, was wearing a
beautific smile and navigating us down the
highway. We heard only soft asphalt and loud
Moody Blues: *"Breathe deep the gathering gloom.*

Watch lights fade from every room ..." The rest of us are absolutely silent. Staring at Connie, staring at the wheel, staring at the road. And each of us is terrified to tell her that she *is* driving – for fear she'll panic, lose control and kill us all. *"Cold hearted orb that rules the night. Removes the colors from our sight. Red is grey and yellow white ..."* I am in the seat next to Connie. Frozen. Uncertain whether to grab the wheel. *"But we decide which one is right. And which is an illusion."*

The miles went by in silence as we barreled through the twilight. And there we sat. Seven panicked faces in a metal box moving seventy miles an hour. And Connie, happy and serene, holding the wheel. Secure in the knowledge that someone else is driving.

(*A LIGHT rises on MAC, sitting at his console. JESSE turns and looks at him.*)

MAC. (*Over his shoulder.*) Let's crack open the scotch, Jesse boy. Whaddya say?

JESSE. I come to work now because I'm afraid who they'll replace me with.

MAC. C'mon Jes. Lighten up.

JESSE. I am terrified that someone else is driving.

MAC. It's ten p.m. We are halfway there.

YOU. As before, YOU imagine an intermission. This time, however, YOU are on your own.

(*A loud, fast BLACKOUT. HOUSE LIGHTS rise. You may want to go to the lobby for something to drink.*)

END OF ACT I

ACT II

(HOUSE LIGHTS flicker, twice.)

YOU. A light flickers. YOU take your seat. As before, the intermission ends. YOU see the Fallout Shelter.

AT RISE: LIGHTS rise on the Fallout Shelter. JESSE stands there, dressed in a brand new uniform. HE is looking at the room.

YOU. YOU see Jesse there. Your mind goes back one year. YOU imagine he has just been assigned to the missile base.

(Silence, as JESSE moves around the room, curious.)

YOU. A large door opens and shuts. Luke arrives.

(SHE does.)

YOU. A moment of social confusion ensues.
LUKE. Hi.

JESSE. Hi.

(*Silence.*)

LUKE. Can I help you?
JESSE. What?
LUKE. Nothing's for sale.
JESSE. I know that. I'm looking.
LUKE. For what?
JESSE. It's a public place. I'm just looking.

(*Silence.*)

LUKE. You here to meet someone?
JESSE. No.
LUKE. You doing reconnaissance?
JESSE. No.
LUKE. You are here to score drugs.

(*JESSE glares at her.*)

LUKE. Look. People just don't come here. They kill their time elsewhere. I know they do. Gum?
JESSE. Do I want some?
LUKE. Do you have some?
JESSE. Uh, no. I don't. I've got a Certs.
LUKE. No gum, huh?
JESSE. No.
LUKE. We are unable to quench primal needs. Maybe we're extinct. It would be just like

this culture to be extinct and not know it. Maybe
the earth long ago asked us to leave, but on the way
out we forgot to unplug our Electronic Devices and
our Home Appliances. Maybe we've been dead for
years, but our own pulse of information keeps us
from lying down. You want to lie down?

(*Silence.*)

JESSE. No. Sorry.

LUKE. Sorry?

JESSE. I usually have gum.

LUKE. Oh. (*Pause.*) I'm Luke.

JESSE. John Randall. Friends call me Jesse.

LUKE. (*Moving to the Quaker Oats box, not
shaking hands.*) Hi, John.

JESSE. What's with the box?

LUKE. (*Simply, as SHE looks for gum
inside.*) Infinity.

JESSE. Pardon me?

LUKE. Our first glimpse of infinity comes
early. At 7:15 on a school morning as we sit in
front of a plastic bowl with oatmeal steam rising
into our face. We hold our spoon and stare at the
Quaker Oats box Mom left on the table. On the
Quaker Oats box is a picture of a man holding a
Quaker Oats box. On the box he is holding is a
picture of a man holding a Quaker Oats box. On
that box is a picture of a man holding a Quaker
Oats box. At 7:15 on a school morning we
understand infinity. At 8 a.m. we open books and

are taught the capital of Vermont. Think about your kids.

YOU. YOU think about your kids.

LUKE. Your kids are immortal, John. Your kids are prime numbers.

JESSE. I don't have any kids.

(*Silence.*)

LUKE. Nice tie.

JESSE. Thanks.

LUKE. What's it mean to you?

JESSE. What?

LUKE. Your tie. What does it mean to you?

JESSE. It's just a tie.

LUKE. I'm sorry to hear that.

YOU. YOU see Luke pity him and hand him a dollar.

JESSE. (*Taking the dollar.*) What's this for?

LUKE. It's what I do. So, you're gonna be a crew dog, huh?

JESSE. A crew —

LUKE. It's lingo. You'll pick it up. Start tomorrow?

JESSE. Yeah.

LUKE. At Dover Zero? The eight to midnight shift with Arthur McCormick?

JESSE. How do you know that?

LUKE. I know the uniform. It's in my blood. This part of the country you're either planting things in the earth or hiding things in the earth. Feed or bleed. Grow or blow, you know?

JESSE. You live around here?

LUKE. I live here. More than a year now. I'm lucky. I got here first. I got Card Number One.

YOU. YOU see Jesse not understand. YOU see Luke step into a spotlight.

LUKE. (*Addressing the audience.*) In the event of of disaster, the first person to arrive in an official United States Department of Civil Defense Fallout Shelter will discover a small manila folder marked "Emergency Shelter Instructions."

(*MR. ANDERSON joins Luke in the SPOTLIGHT. HE is dressed as the FEMA employee we saw earlier. HE carries a clipboard and a small shovel. HE hands Luke a 5x7 manila folder.*)

LUKE. Thank you, Mr. Anderson.

MR. ANDERSON. (*Your favorite uncle.*) My pleasure, Luke.

LUKE. Inside this folder are a number of white instruction cards, numbered One through Ten. The person who discovers the folder gets Card Number One. Card Number One welcomes its holder to the Shelter and proclaims its holder the SHELTER LEADER. The SHELTER LEADER is responsible for the distribution of cards Two through Ten. These cards put other

Shelter inhabitants in charge of the various Shelter functions:

MR. ANDERSON. Food, water, first aid, radiation detection. Other stuff.

LUKE. All of these "Captains" – if you will – must report to the SHELTER LEADER on a regular basis.

(*MR. ANDERSON points to something on LUKE's card.*)

LUKE. Thank you, Mr. Anderson.

MR. ANDERSON. My pleasure, Luke.

LUKE. Most importantly, the SHELTER LEADER determines when the Shelter is FULL. When this has been determined, Card Number One states *emphatically* that NO ONE –

MR. ANDERSON. UNDER ANY CIR-CUMSTANCES –

LUKE. BE ALLOWED TO ENTER. Individuals pounding on the doors are to be instructed to seek shelter elsewhere. Sufficient shelter is available for the entire population if properly distributed. Mr. Anderson, is there anything you'd like to add?

MR. ANDERSON. Just this, Luke. In the midst of most certain chaos and annihilation outside, a lovely little totalitarian society will begin to blossom inside. A common citizen may be elevated, by pure happenstance, to *Dictator*. Who knows, you may be that lucky person.

YOU. The spotlight disappears.

(*IT does.*)

JESSE. What are you talking about? There are no supplies here. There's *nothing* here.
YOU. The spotlight reappears.

(*IT does.*)

MR. ANDERSON. It's an oversight.
LUKE. They'll get to it.
MR. ANDERSON. The supplies for the city of (*name of your city*) have been safely stored in a downtown warehouse since 1971. The Federal Emergency Management Agency has yet to determine whether – in the unlikely event of nuclear war – the populace should be housed in the existing shelters within the city, or be transported by bus or train to one huge shelter in the countryside. As soon as this is determined, the appropriate shelters will be stocked. Including the shelter nearest this theatre at (*give location of nearest Shelter*). Thanks for your interest and have a great day.
YOU. The spotlight disappears.

(*IT does. MR. ANDERSON is gone.*)

LUKE. Hi.
JESSE. I can't believe there's nothing here.

LUKE. Yeah, it's kind of minimal, but not as minimal as my dad. You're terrified.

JESSE. What?

LUKE. I can hear your heart. Say the Oath. Say it with me. Maybe that'll help. "I understand the responsibilities of missile combat crew member and –" Don't you know this?

JESSE. I know it.

LUKE. I don't believe you. "I understand the responsibilities of missile combat crew member and realize what actions –

JESSE. (*Joining in.*)
"––what actions this duty may entail. I certify that I have no reservations over my ability and my conviction to perform in such a capacity."

LUKE.
"—this duty may entail. I certify that I have no reservations over ..." (*Stops.*)

(*Silence.*)

LUKE. Better?

JESSE. They designated this a Shelter. In our training we were told that various fortified buildings had been chosen as —

LUKE. A place to run?

JESSE. That sufficient shelter was avail–

LUKE. There's nowhere to run.

JESSE. How can they call this a *Shelter?*
LUKE. Empty, it is a Shelter. Full, it's a tomb.

(*Silence.*)

JESSE. Then what are you doing here?
LUKE. The time now is ten-oh-six. Mr. Leon Glass has buried a time capsule in his yard. It contains only lipstick and travelers' checks.
JESSE. What the hell is *that?*
LUKE. It's what I'm doing here. I'm trying to think beyond the room I'm in. How 'bout you?

(*Silence. JESSE stares at her, motionless.*)

YOU. YOU see Jesse turn and leave. YOU imagine the passing of a year. YOU see Jesse return.
LUKE. Hi.
JESSE. Hi.
LUKE. Nice tie.
JESSE. (*Holding out hand immediately.*) I don't know what it means.
LUKE. (*Hands him a dollar.*) You forget something?
JESSE. No.
LUKE. You came back.
JESSE. (*Offering her a stick.*) Gum?
LUKE. Thank you.

JESSE. Tell me what you know about McCormick. You knew they assigned me to his shift. How?

(*Silence.*)

LUKE. Arthur McCormick used to be my Dad. On the last day he was my dad, Arthur McCormick gave me a combination lock. I put it on my bike. When I thanked him, he told me the lock had belonged to his partner, William Brady.

(*LIGHTS rise on the Command Post as LUKE speaks. MAC sits at his console. A FIGURE in a military hat and uniform sits at Jesse's console. The FIGURE's back is to the audience. During the following, LUKE leads JESSE into the Command Post. The men in the Command Post do not see LUKE and JESSE.*)

LUKE. It seems Brady was unable to come to work anymore. It seems he was being replaced by a young man named John. Friends call him Jesse. I have pieced the story together. It turns out it wasn't really McCormick's fault. He's a normal guy. He got bored staring at the monitors hour after night, night after year. He tired of the dull hum of the Monopoly and the monotony of the room. He decided he wanted to play with the keys. You know. The keys. Brady tried to distract him with scotch. No luck. The keys. Brady tried to distract him with Miss February. No luck. The keys. Brady wanted no part of McCormick's plan. (Not because he was a stickler for rules, but because he had *hotels* on Boardwalk and Park Place and McCormick was heading straight for that deep blue.) McCormick stood up. He went to the little red safe.

YOU. Luke shows YOU the little red safe.

LUKE. He started working the locks to get at the keys. Brady, suspecting his partner of sabotage, followed orders and drew his gun. McCormick spun on his heel and put a bullet through Brady's skull with his M-15.

MAC. (*Over his shoulder, to the Figure.*) So whaddya say, Jes?

LUKE. I rode my bike to Mittendorf and Sons. I'd never been to a funeral before. I wondered why there were no women pallbearers. I wrote my Mom — Indiana, General Delivery — and asked if she'd ever seen a woman pallbearer. She wrote me back a four word letter. "Women birth. Men bury."

MAC. C'mon, it's after ten. I am ready to *celebrate*.

JESSE. There must have been some action taken.

LUKE. Yes. They replaced him with you.

(*JESSE turns and stands, facing front. LUKE speaks to him during the following.*)

YOU. Jesse runs home to hide. Luke is there.

LUKE. The time now is ten ten. A little boy, looking in his attic for a toy, has instead found a flag. The flag is flying him.

YOU. Jesse runs to a bar to hide. Luke is there.

LUKE. It may dawn on that man this evening – why don't I think beyond the room I'm in?

YOU. Jesse runs to a church to hide. Luke is there.

LUKE. It may dawn on that man this evening – why don't I think beyond the room I'm in?

YOU. Jesse runs to a health club to hide. Luke is there.

LUKE. It may dawn on thatmanand thatmanandthatman this evening – whydon'tIdwhydon'tI think beyond the room I'm in?

YOU. Jesse runs to graduate school to hide. Luke is there.

LUKE. The time has come to ask questions.

YOU. Jesse runs to the missile silo to hide. Luke is there.

LUKE. Who is taking stock and who is asleep at the wheel?

JESSE. (*Still facing front.*) There are two kinds of crazy people: People who are crazy, and people who are FUCKING crazy. You are *both*.

YOU. Jesse runs and tries to hide in all the places where he put things and never had to think of them again. Luke is there.

LUKE. (*Simply.*) Stay.

(*Silence. JESSE stares front. Then, JESSE turns and looks at LUKE. After a moment, HE turns front and addresses the audience. Calm. Confident.*)

JESSE. Change is quicksilver. It can happen in a word. And I hate it. I hate it when it happens. I hate to change and I hate to learn. It hurts me. It disrupts my days. Change is like a psychological paper cut: it is not just something you hate — it is *precisely* what you hate. I've changed my thinking before. I show the scars at parties during the holidays. It can be instantaneous. It can happen in a word. People who say otherwise have never changed, and do not believe them if they tell you they have.

I used to have a friend named Henry. We used to live in an old house in a college town. Me, Henry, and about eight of our friends. One day, all of us in the house somehow became *convinced* that Henry was going to kill himself. All of us in the house began to take action to protect Henry from the inevitable. We emptied the knives from the drawers. We kept him off the roof. We stole his belts and kept no rope in the house. We refused to let him drive and we never, ever left him all alone. Henry, for his part, had *absolutely no desire* to kill himself. Paying no attention to this fact, we persisted. At first, Henry was bemused by our efforts. Then curious. Then confused. Eventually, our paranoia overcame him. By this time, however, all of us in the house had become lax and assumed that it was a false alarm. We were proud of our efforts. We were happy and relieved. It can happen in a word. We all left Henry at home one night to go to a concert. As we were leaving, I poked my head back inside the door, smiled and said: "Henry, you gonna be okay here?" He said: "You tell me. How do *you* think I'll be?" I said: "Fine."

It can happen in a word. Fine. Soon. Sorry. Yes. Never. Careful. Trust. Always. Words. Paper cuts. And change is part of the bloodletting.

A word is spoken and suddenly I will have known her for years.

LUKE. Stay.

(LUKE and JESSE walk toward each other.)

JESSE. John Randall.
LUKE. *(Smiles.)* I know.
JESSE. Friends call me –
LUKE. Hello, Jesse.
YOU. YOU imagine they have known each other for years.

(*LUKE and JESSE embrace. LUKE sits on the floor. JESSE kneels behind her and massages her neck and shoulders during the following.*)

LUKE. What am I thinking? Go.
JESSE. You are thinking simultaneously about John Lennon, nuclear winter, pet turtles and St. Patrick's Day. Go.
LUKE. You are thinking simultaneously about neckties. Ground Zero, Willie Mays, and root beer floats. Go.
JESSE. Buddy Holly and bowling pins. Go.
LUKE. Beethoven and the Boland Amendment. Go.
JESSE. Easter Sunday and your turquoise yo-yo. Go.
LUKE. Your German shepherd. Go.
JESSE. Your Monkees albums. Go.
LUKE. Your Elvis-on-Velvet. Go.
JESSE. Your fear of heights. Go.
LUKE. Your fear of driving. Go.
JESSE. Your fear of commitment. Go.
LUKE. Your fear of solitude. Go.
JESSE. Your fear of marriage. Go.
LUKE. Your fear of children. Go.
JESSE. Your fear of becoming a McParent.
YOU. YOU imagine Luke as a parent, years later.

(*LUKE moves to the down right chair.*)

YOU. Go.

LUKE. I imagine you and I in our conservative townhouse community. Manicured lawns and a thousand points of light. I have caught Gregory having an affair with an alderman. I have treated him like a bad day in the Old Testament, filed for divorce, and tossed him out. His clothes fit you perfectly. You and I run away to each other. We begin as total strangers. Become friendly strangers. Become intimate strangers. We are desirous of a legacy. We test our blood and sign our will between the sheets. We penetrate each other and clutter the earth with tiny, educable entities. We welcome them with early warnings. Gifts are lavished. Names are composed. We feed then video valium and dress them like magazines. We monitor their rooms with cameras. We converse through intercoms. We spank through neglect. Our children grow and grow until they overtake us. They pity us. They place us in their homes on doilies and dust us weekly. They put granite near our heads and toss flowers on our stomachs. Our clothes fit them perfectly.

(*Silence.*)

JESSE. What time is it?

(*Silence.*)

JESSE. Luke. What time is it? (*Silence. JESSE moves closer to her.*) Tell me.

LUKE. (*Stands.*) The time now is eleven eleven.

MAC. (*Over his shoulder, to the Figure.*) C'mon, Jes. Get with the *program.*

JESSE. A woman stands and remembers that her kids will be immortal.

(*LUKE removes a white tie which we haven't seen before from around her neck. SHE places it around Jesse's neck during the following.*)

MAC. Take a hit of this. It ain't Chivas, but it's brown. C'mon, Jes. *Play* with me. I got Miss February here, and for a short month she's got awful long legs.

LUKE. Keep this.

MAC. You know, Jes. It's time.

(*JESSE turns and starts to leave.*)

LUKE. And don't let Mac get all the railroads or he'll kill you.

MAC. It's high time you did it.

(*JESSE is gone.*)

MAC. It's time you got married. It's time you put on a clean shirt, went out, roped and broke yourself a filly and saddled yourself with a mortgage. It's time you made that *one great phone call*. Christ, you're quiet tonight, Jes. You know I hate quiet. Well, if you're not gonna talk to me, at least get over here and play the game. It's your turn, old boy.

(*The FIGURE turns. It is MR. ANDERSON wearing the uniform that Luke wore earlier. It fits him perfectly. HE also wears a very authentic-looking mustache.*)

MR. ANDERSON. (*Very gregarious.*) M y *turn?* Christ, Mac – I just bought Park Place and two hotels. It's *your* turn.

(*MAC stares at him.*)

MR. ANDERSON. You can hog the magazine, buddy – but don't Bogart the bottle.

(*MAC slowly hands him the bottle. MR. ANDERSON drinks.*)

MR. ANDERSON. Christ, you gotta stop this Everclear and food coloring shit.
    MAC. Brady?
    MR. ANDERSON. What?
    MAC. *Brady?*
    MR. ANDERSON. (*Imitating.*) *Mac?*
    MAC. Is that you, Brady?

MR. ANDERSON. Is that you, Mac? Or some other asshole stalling for time? You're headin' straight for that deep blue. There's no way around it. I got two hotels on each. Now, roll the God. Damn. Dice.

YOU. YOU see Mac roll the dice, looking only at Brady.

MR. ANDERSON. Shit! You wily old sonofabitch! You roll doubles and you land on GO. You are a warrior, Mac. Beneath those dull eyes is the genius of a caged animal.

YOU. YOU see Mac talk to Brady, looking only at the dice.

MAC. Brady?

MR. ANDERSON. How's you daughter, Mac?

MAC. Fine.

MR. ANDERSON. What's her name again?

MAC. Linda.

MR. ANDERSON. Get her to sleep upstairs, yet?

MAC. No.

MR. ANDERSON. Ever hear from your wife?

MAC. No.

MR. ANDERSON. Well, Indiana's a fine place.

MAC. Yeah?

MR. ANDERSON. Race cars, family farms and basketball.

MAC. Don't say.

MR. ANDERSON. Yeah. An Indiana basketball hit me square in the face when I was eight years old.

MAC. No shit.

MR. ANDERSON. Hell, you think I got this ugly on my *own?*

(Silence.)

MAC. How's your farm?

MR. ANDERSON. Had predators last week.

MAC. Shoot 'em?

MR. ANDERSON. No. Bought me a watchdog.

MAC. Doberman?

MR. ANDERSON. 'Course. Anything else is just a *pet.*

MAC. Name it?

MR. ANDERSON. *Name* it? Hell, I don't even *feed* it. You gonna waste those doubles or you gonna roll?

YOU. Mac looks Brady in the face.

MAC. Jesse?

MR. ANDERSON. What?

MAC. Jesse?

MR. ANDERSON. *Jesse?*

MAC. Yeah.

MR. ANDERSON. Jesse!

MAC. Yeah!

MR. ANDERSON. Hell. I thought sure it was Ginger. I'd a swore it was Ginger or Gina you

liked. Or Gretchen. Heather. Maybe Heidi. I
didn't know about any Jesse. Must be a new girl.
You must've made that *one great phone call* and
had some fun without me. You're a date machine,
Mac. You're an animal waitin' to happen. Want
to use your card or mine? Kidding. I'm kidding. I
know it's my turn. Just a joke, Mac. Christ,
lighten up. You look like a goddamn *eclipse*.

MAC. *Brady?*

MR. ANDERSON. Yeah. *Jesse.* I know. I've
got it.

YOU. YOU see Brady dial a number which is
written on the back of his tie. Line 6 lights up.
YOU answer it.

MR. ANDERSON. (*To Mac.*) I got through.

YOU. (*Business-like.*) Hello.

MR. ANDERSON. Hi. How you doin'
tonight?

YOU. Would you like a call?

MR. ANDERSON. Yes.

YOU. Have you used our service before?

MR. ANDERSON. Oh, yes.

YOU. Major credit card?

MR. ANDERSON. Yes.

YOU. Is your phone number listed under the
name as it appears on your card?

MR. ANDERSON. Yes, it is.

YOU. Fine. For twenty-five dollars you can
talk to a sexy girl of your choice for up to twelve
minutes. Like to give it a try?

MR. ANDERSON. The call is for commander Arthur McCormick.

YOU. Arthur. Fine. Your name as it appears on your card?

MR. ANDERSON. William J. Brady.

MAC. *Bill?*

MR. ANDERSON. *(To Mac.) Jesse.* I know.

YOU. Card number?

MR. ANDERSON. Master Card 5476 - 1800-6543-2425.

YOU. Expiration date?

MR. ANDERSON. Eleven eighty-nine.

YOU. Phone. Area code first.

MR. ANDERSON. 801-263-8623. Extension 6606.

YOU. In what publication did you see our ad?

MR. ANDERSON. Christ, we've been calling for years – I don't even remember.

YOU. Fine. What kind of girl would you like tonight? Sensuous, hot and sexy, kinky, dominant, nymphomaniac, bisexual –

MR. ANDERSON. Is Jesse there?

MAC. Is that you, Billy?

YOU. We have a Jackie and a Janet tonight. No Jesse. What kind of girl is she? Sensuous, hot and sexy, kinky, dom –

MR. ANDERSON. Look. I don't care who calls. Just have 'em *say* they're Jesse. Okay?

YOU. Fine.

MR. ANDERSON. And make 'em dominant.

YOU. Fine. A sexy girl will call you back collect in the next ten minutes.

MR. ANDERSON. Thanks so much.

YOU. Goodnight.

MR. ANDERSON. (*Hanging up the phone.*) You're in, old man. It's all over but the wakin' up. You get done with Jesse and still have some blood in your legs, maybe you and me can crack open that safe and play with those keys. Whaddya say?

YOU. YOU imagine that six minutes and five seconds have passed.

(*Amplified sound of PHONE RINGING.*)

MR. ANDERSON. (*Laughing.*) Don't be shy, old man. Somebody wants you bad.

(*PHONE keeps ringing.*)

MR. ANDERSON. You better buck up, old friend, or that babe is gonna leave you for dead.

(*PHONE keeps ringing.*)

MR. ANDERSON. Never know, Mac. Might be your wife.

MAC. (*Picks up the phone immediately.*) McCormick. What? Yes. I'll accept.

(*A shaft of BACKLIGHT on LUKE in the Fallout Shelter.*)

LUKE. Hello. Is this Arthur?

MAC. Yes.

LUKE. Arthur, this is Jesse. How you doin'?

MAC. (*Softly.*) Fine.

LUKE. What did you have in mind for me tonight?

MAC. Uh ... I ... uh –

LUKE. Have you been a bad boy?

MAC. Uh –

LUKE. Did you clean your room?

MAC. No.

LUKE. Should I punish you?

MAC. Uh –

LUKE. Talk to me, Arthur. Have you been bad?

MAC. Yes.

LUKE. Do I need to punish you?

MAC. Yes.

LUKE. I can't hear you. You are all the way in the basement. Get up here.

MAC. I, uh –

LUKE. Are you upstairs now?

MAC. Yes.

LUKE. I can't hear you.

MAC. *Yes.* I am.

LUKE. You are *what?*

MAC. Upstairs.

LUKE. Are you on the rug in the front room?

MAC. Yes.

LUKE. Have you lit a fire?

MAC. Yes.

LUKE. Have you poured me some hot chocolate?

MAC. Yes.

LUKE. Have you covered me with a blanket?

MAC. Yes.

LUKE. Are you sorry you were bad?

MAC. Yes.

LUKE. Will you do anything to make it better?

MAC. Yes.

LUKE. *Anything?*

MAC. Yes.

LUKE. Swear to me.

MAC. I swear.

LUKE. I want it now.

MAC. Yes.

LUKE. I want you to make it better.

MAC. Yes.

LUKE. I want you to do what I say.

MAC. Yes.

LUKE. Now.

MAC. Yes.

LUKE. Right now.

MAC. Yes.

LUKE. Tell me the story of Bob.

(*Silence.*)

MAC. Plumbbob.

LUKE. Right. *Plumbbob.* Operation Plumbbob.
MAC. Yes.
LUKE. Tell it to me.
MAC. Yes.
LUKE. Tell it to me now.

(*Silence. The BACKLIGHT on LUKE has shifted to FRONTLIGHT, gradually. We see HER watch MAC during the following.*)

MAC. On a lovely day in June, 1957, there was a young army soldier stationed in Nevada. This soldier was named Arthur.

(*Silence.*)

LUKE. Do not stop.

(*Silence.*)

MAC. Arthur was a 23 year old enlisted man who had been assigned to participate in the Atmospheric Nuclear Weapons Test series. This series of tests in the Nevada desert was code named Plumbbob.
LUKE. Do not stop.
MAC. From 1946 to 1951, the United States military had conducted nuclear tests in the Pacific Marshall Islands, but it was their avid

hope to move the tests closer to home. The reason was twofold: it was cheaper and easier.

On June 18th, 1957, a 10-kiloton bomb was to be exploded in the Nevada desert. The military hoped to measure the explosive capacity of the bomb, the radiation released, and the effect of this radiation on American servicemen. The radiation was given a code name as well. This name was "Wilson."

LUKE. Do not stop.

MAC. Some servicemen were assigned to view the blast from airplanes. Others viewed it from land at a distance of eight miles from Ground Zero. Still another group of servicemen – volunteers – viewed the blast from trenches at a distance of 500 feet. Arthur was one of these volunteers.

He put on the dark glasses he had been assigned. On the recommendation of the soldier next to him, he applied suntan lotion to his face and neck. He put his helmet on his head and crawled down into the trench. His eyes focused on a balloon which was suspended 500 feet above the ground.

LUKE. Yes.

MAC. Inside the balloon was the bomb.

LUKE. Yes.

MAC. As the countdown proceeded, Arthur was thinking simultaneously about Hank Williams, Hiroshima, lawn chairs and the girl that got away.

LUKE. Yes.

MAC. At 4:45 a.m. the bomb exploded. A portion of Arthur exploded along with it. The heat made his skin retreat and the fireball made his eyes narrow. Squinting hard and waving the smoke from his face, he struggled to watch the cloud ascend. The light engulfed him. It was a light that had God in it. And peace. And death. It was a light that went through his body like a prism, leaving shards of "Wilson" in its wake. Arthur rose to his feet in the trench and watched the afterglow.

LUKE. Stop.

MAC. He was 23 years old and he had seen a billion-year-old secret be released.

LUKE. Stop.

MAC. He was smoldering and terrified and immortal. From that day on, Arthur wore this explosion. It dangled from his life like dice.

LUKE. Daddy, stop.

MAC. Through the years, blinding white light haunted him. The glare of headlights and the flash of cameras brought back that lovely Nevada day in 1957.

LUKE. Please, Daddy –

MAC. And the shards left in his body haunted him as well. Arthur had God in him. And peace. And death. Little pieces of his head kept falling out.

(*Silence.*)

LUKE. Goodbye, Daddy.

(*Silence. LIGHTS out on LUKE. MR. ANDERSON is standing near the safe, playing with the locks.*)

YOU. YOU see Brady fiddling with the locks on the little red safe. YOU see Mac slowly draw his gun.

MAC. (*Advancing on Mr. Anderson.*) I know you and your goddamn ticks. I KNOW THAT'S YOU, BRADY, AND I AM TIRED OF YOUR –

MR. ANDERSON. (*Turning, removing hat and mustache.*) *Anderson*. Mr. Anderson. Don't sweat it. I'm terrible with names, too. Look, I just want to thank you once again for the guided tour. It was *absolutely lifelike*. Just like the brochure promised. From my entire family, sir – thank you. You've made this vacation a vacation to remember. (*MR.ANDERSON is gone.*)

YOU. YOU see Mac comb his hair. Repeatedly.

MR. ANDERSON. (*Reappears.*) Oh, by the by, do you have the time?

MAC. The time now is eleven thirty-seven.

LUKE. Billy White has called an exterminator because something has died inside her walls.

MR. ANDERSON. Thanks so much. (*MR. ANDERSON is gone.*)

YOU. YOU see Mac realize he is alone in the Command Post. This has never happened.

(*Silence. MAC looks around the room. HE combs his hair. Finally, HE speaks to the audience.*)

MAC. I don't like the quiet.
Once. Once at breakfast with my wife. Once at breakfast with my wife it was so quiet that I could hear her cigarette burn.
I don't like the quiet. The quiet makes me think I should be doing something. (*Stares front. Puts the comb away. Swivels his chair and stares at the little red safe. Pauses. Then, rushes toward the safe and begins working the locks.*)

(*Simultaneously, very loud sound of a DOORBELL.*)

MAC. (*Immediately stops what he's doing.*) Come in.

(*JESSE walks quickly into the Command Post wearing the white tie and carrying a Boston fern. HE places the fern in the midst of the Monopoly game.*)

JESSE. Hello, Mac.
MAC. Jes?
JESSE. There's plenty of light, Mac. It'll be fine.

MAC. Where've you been, Jes?

JESSE. I found your daughter.

MAC. Her name's not Linda.

JESSE. She's living in a Fallout Shelter.

YOU. YOU remember that your nearest shelter is at (*give location of nearest shelter.*)

MAC. Find my wife, too?

JESSE. No.

MAC. Nice tie.

JESSE. Thanks. Luke told me what happened to Brady.

MAC. You got the time?

JESSE. The time now is eleven thirty-nine.

LUKE. A woman in Denver just discovered that if you look at your husband the wrong way you will stop loving him.

MAC. Got any gum, Jes?

JESSE. You were trying to play with the keys.

MAC. Gum?

JESSE. Brady pulled his gun to stop you.

MAC. Certs?

JESSE. And he wasn't unmarked for long.

MAC. (*Combing hair.*) You got no proof at all.

JESSE. Your hair looks fine.

MAC. You gotta believe me, Jes. You must always believe your commanding officer or the system will break down.

(*Three huge KNOCKS, amplified.*)

MAC.   JESSE.
COME IN!   GO AWAY!

(*MR. ANDERSON appears in a bear mask,
waving a Soviet flag and holding a plastic
Halloween pumpkin.*)

MR. ANDERSON. TRICK OR TREAT,
TRICK OR TREAT, MR ANDERSON HAS
FOUND YOUR STREET!
MAC.   JESSE.
GO AWAY!   COME IN!

(*MR. ANDERSON is gone. LUKE holds a tire
pump and a deflated football. With each of her
lines during the following, SHE adds air to
the football– until it is completely inflated.*)

LUKE. We hold these truths to be self-evident.
JESSE. You lied to me about Brady just like
you lied to me about Delgado.
MAC. I know for a fact –
JESSE. I know for a fact that Delgado did not
give you my combination.
LUKE. That all men are created equal.
JESSE. I swore him to secrecy.
MAC. Then ask me what it is.
JESSE. No.
MAC. Go on. Ask me what you combo is.

YOU. Jesse is silent.

MAC. This is an order, Randall. Ask your C.O. what your combo is.

LUKE. That they are endowed by their Creator with certain unalienable rights.

MAC. That could get you fired, Jes.

JESSE. Fine.

LUKE. That among these are life.

MAC. No pension, either.

LUKE. Liberty.

JESSE. Wonderful.

LUKE. And the pursuit of happiness.

MAC. The first number is the year the market crashed.

LUKE. That to secure these rights.

MAC. The second number is the day after Independence.

LUKE. Governments are instituted among men.

MAC. The third number is what Judas was paid.

LUKE. Deriving their powers from the consent of the governed.

MAC. 29 - 5 - 30.

LUKE. That whenever any form of government becomes destructive to these ends.

MAC. Those numbers are right, aren't they, Jes?

LUKE. It is the responsibility of the people to alter or abolish it.

MAC. I've landed on FREE PARKING, haven't I?

LUKE. And to institute a new government.

MAC. If you won't admit I'm right, I'LL GO TO THAT LOCK AND SHOW YOU. (*Starts for the lock.*)

JESSE. I know your combo, too.

(*MAC stops.*)

LUKE. Laying its foundation on such principles and organizing its powers in such form.

MAC. You what?

JESSE. I've known for a year.

LUKE. As to them shall seem most likely.

MAC. Bullhshit.

JESSE. 17 - 20 - 11.

LUKE. To affect their safety and happiness.

(*LUKE throws the football to YOU. Startled, YOU catch it.*)

MAC. You're an evil man, John Randall.

JESSE. And you're my superior.

MAC. Who squealed my combo to you?

JESSE. Nobody.

MAC. Was it Luke?

JESSE. No. It's written on the back of your tie.

(*Silence.*)

MAC. You are no longer a good soldier, Jes. You have forgotten your oath. Say it with me, Jes. "I UNDERSTAND THE RESPONSIBILITIES OF MISSILE COMBAT CREW MEMBER AND REALIZE WHAT ACTIONS THIS DUTY MAY ENTAIL."

LUKE. Dad.

MAC. Not now, honey. "I CERTIFY THAT I HAVE NO RESERVATIONS OVER MY ABILITY –"

LUKE. Dad.

MAC. "– AND MY CONVICTION TO PERFORM IN SUCH A CAPACITY."

LUKE. You scare me, Daddy.

MAC. (*Turning to Luke.*) What?

LUKE. I think there are people that should never be given weapons and I think those people all look like you.

MAC. Luke –

LUKE. Bye, Dad. I left a note for you in the basement.

(*LUKE takes a program for the play out of the quaker Oats box and drops it to the ground in the Fallout Shelter.*)

YOU. YOU imagine Mac walking down into the basement of his modest, inner-city home. As he does this, Luke turns and looks at YOU.

(*MAC moves into the Shelter and finds the program. LUKE moves close to YOU.*)

YOU. YOU don't know what she wants. YOU don't want to be singled out. YOU try to dismiss her. YOU read from your program.

"We drove home in silence. *Survive* was performed once, then disappeared. David moved to New York. I put Luke in a file. Several years passed."

(*LUKE begins putting her ties, one by one, around YOUR neck.*)

YOU. "I was in a Minneapolis church listening to Helen Caldicott give a lecture on the medical effects of nuclear war. She spoke eloquently, without emotion, for an hour. She spoke clinically about the earth as a patient affected with nuclear fallout as a disease. She was factual, brutal and persuasive. Then, in the last line of her speech, she said:

JESSE. (*Reading from a program he has pulled from his notebook.*) "And, finally, I am a mother with children. And let me tell you this: *nobody* harms my kids."

YOU. "This moment was followed, weeks later, by an event that seemed somehow perfectly related. My President, unaware that a radio mike was on, made a joke:"

MAC. (*Reading the program Luke left in the Shelter.*) "My fellow Americans, I'm pleased to tell you today that I've signed legislation that will outlaw Russia forever. We begin bombing in five minutes."

YOU. "That same year, Vice President George Bush said:

MAC. "Some people believe there can be no such thing as a winner in a nuclear war. But I don't believe that."

YOU. (*Standing.*) "My generation –"

JESSE. "The kids who had crawled under their desks during Civil Defense drills in elementary school –"

YOU. "Had now, as adults –"

JESSE. "Elected a man who named the MX missile the 'Peacekeeper'."

YOU. "The unthinkable was now the commonplace."

(*LUKE sits in YOUR chair and speaks into the mike.*)

LUKE. The time now is eleven fifty-five.

YOU. "We are hounded now by technology –"

MAC. "That like Mr. Anderson –"

YOU. "Will not go away."

JESSE. "We attempt futuristic solutions to primitive problems."

YOU. "We cherish laughter and look extinction in the eye."

JESSE. "We are playing Frisbee in the graveyard."

LUKE. YOU ARE HERE.

YOU. "Infinity continues to look to us all."

LUKE. End of story.

(*A SIREN is heard. Soft, from a distance.*)

MAC. (*Drops the program.*) What the hell is that?

YOU. YOU hear a very distant siren.

(*MAC rushes back into the Command Post. YOU move into the Fallout shelter, wearing the ties, carrying the football.*)

YOU. YOU hear the siren gradually grow louder from this point to the end of the play. The control monitors light up. YOU see them.

MAC. Happy Anniversary, Jes! It's time to pay the fiddler.

LUKE. The time now is eleven fifty-seven. Gracie is pounding at the door. She is trying to say goodnight.

(*An ALARM SOUNDS in the Command Post. Very loud.*)

MAC. This is an order, Jes.

JESSE. "I am not proud of these days, but they reside in me."

MAC. What the hell is THAT?
JESSE. My autobiography.

(*ALARM SOUNDS.*)

MAC. This is an order you cannot ignore.
JESSE. "These are the days I first bordered on destruction. These are the days I flirted with murder."
MAC. THE OTHER SHIFT'LL BE HERE IN THREE MINUTES –
JESSE. "And insurgency."
MAC. AND I DID NOT SIT IN THIS SILO ALL THESE YEARS –
JESSE. "And genocide."
MAC. TO LET SOME OTHER GUYS HAVE ALL THE FUN.
JESSE. "And deceit."

(*MAC pulls his gun and points it at JESSE.*)

MAC. I don't need your bullshit, partner. I just need your fingers turning a key.

(*ALARM SOUNDS.*)

MAC. Now, read off that code.
LUKE. The time now is eleven fifty-eight.
JESSE. (*Reads the incoming code from his console and transcribes it.*) Eagle.
MAC. (*Doing the same.*) Eagle.

LUKE. A virgin puts a pitcher of beer to her lips.

JESSE. Bravo.

MAC. Bravo.

LUKE. She stands in her sweat.

JESSE. Romeo.

MAC. Romeo.

LUKE. Wiping the dance from her brow.

JESSE. Alpha.

MAC. Alpha.

LUKE. She is the product of generations –

JESSE. October.

MAC. October.

LUKE. – who have been kicking and clawing their way into the culture.

MAC. We have a VALID MESSAGE, old buddy. This is the real thing. Now, get your ass to that safe.

(*ALARM SOUNDS. JESSE does not move. MAC puts the gun to JESSE's temple.*)

MAC. You can help me open the safe or I can open your fucking head. NOW, GET OVER THERE.

(*THEY move to the little red safe. Three huge KNOCKS, amplified.*)

MAC.	JESSE.
GO AWAY!	COME IN!

(*MR. ANDERSON appears, wearing a raggedy black trenchcoat and carrying a tattered black umbrella. MAC and JESSE ignore him.*)

MR. ANDERSON. MR. ANDERSON'S *UM*BRELLAS. THE SHIELD THAT WILL PROTECT YOU. BE SAFE AND BE HAPPY WITH MR. ANDERSON'S *UM*BRELLAS.

MAC. You seem to have forgotten some things, my friend.

MR. ANDERSON. JUST ONE DEADLY DROP. SPREAD THROUGH YOUR BODY. SPREAD THROUGH YOUR FAMILY.

MAC. You seem to be lacking basic information.

MR. ANDERSON. *UM*BRELLAS. A BARGAIN AT TWICE THE PRICE.

MAC. *Nobody,* Jes.

MR. ANDERSON. YOURS FOR ONLY 29 - 5 - 30.

MAC. Nobody builds a toy and doesn't play with it.

MR. ANDERSON. COMPARE AT 17 - 20 - 11.

(*ALARM SOUNDS.*)

LUKE.

It may dawn on these people this evening – tonight there will be a sort of pause.

MR. ANDERSON.

REGULAR 29 - 5 - 30. TODAY FOR YOU AND YOU ALONE 17 - 20 - 11. WE'VE GOT IT ALL.

LUKE.

It may dawn on these people this evening – tonight at midnight there will be a sort of pause.
It may dawn on thesepeopleandthese peopleandthesepeople – THE TIME NOW IS ELEVEN FIFTY- NINE.

MR. ANDERSON

WE'VE GOT HOTELS ON BOARDWALK AND PARK PLACE AND IT'S HALLOWEEN LIKE YOU'VE NEVER SEEN IT'S THE SALE OF A LIFETIME. IT'S THE DEAL OF THE CENTURY. SAY IT WITH ME ONE AND ALL: 17- 20 - 11! 29 - 5 - 30!

(*ALARM SOUNDS.*)

MAC. Now, work that dial.

(*MAC and JESSE work their dials. MAC's gun
remains trained on JESSE.*
*MR. ANDERSON stands now in the Fallout
Shelter, staring at the audience. YOU stand in
center of the Fallout Shelter, holding the
football and the Quaker Oats box.*)

LUKE. (*Into mike, a rush of information.*)
A woman wears blue pumps on the Avenue
sharpening her heels
on the whetstone street
she is piercing pavement with stride
and hearts with glance
    MAC.
17.
    JESSE.
29.
    LUKE.
A woman hears blue pumps on wet legs
do a Morse code shuffle
and stumble past
eyes that raise and eaves that drop
    MAC.
20.
    JESSE.
5.
    LUKE.
A woman hears a tree rustle under concrete rain

and the footsteps
echo down a stairway someone littered with glass
the night
Vietnam stole the late show
    MAC. Last number, Jes. Turn it.
    LUKE.
She hears clouds spit fire.
    MAC. *Now.*
    LUKE.
She hears the telephone left off the hook
scream in harmony
with the mother who finds the TV is watching her
    kids
and the babysitter is watching her husband
    MAC.
11.
    LUKE.
And it all comes tumbling down the family tree
as the littlest one
who hasn't learned to talk and never will
hangs up the phone and puts one finger inside her
    cheek
to make a popping sound
that reminds her of the movies she went to that
    afternoon
where it was dark
    JESSE.
    30.
    LUKE. And Daddy giggled when the
babysitter crossed her legs.

YOU. YOU see Mac and Jesse open the little red safe.

LUKE. The time is now midnight.

YOU. YOU see Mac check the authenticator.

MAC. Eagle Bravo Romeo Alpha October.

LUKE. The time now is midnight.

MAC. Get your key. NOW.

(ALARM SOUNDS. The MEN take their keys from the safe. THEY move to their consoles, keys poised. MAC keeps the gun trained on JESSE.)

LUKE.
The time now is midnight
and Adam and Eve are on their honeymoon
making love in a room as still as a library
where every movement
shatters the silence
and quickens the heart
and the scream wants out and the library won't let
    it
and the scream wants out and the body won't let it
and the scream wants out
but it will never be heard

YOU. YOU see Mac and Jesse insert their keys.

LUKE. Only felt.

MAC. That key feels *good* in your hand, don't it?

LUKE. Like a forty-five caliber caress.

MAC. Feels *right*.

LUKE. The time now is –

MAC. NOW, Jesse boy. Now, let's DO IT. HANDS ON KEY. ON MY MARK. THREE ... TWO ... ONE –

LUKE. DADDY, I HEARD THE BELL!

MAC. (*Turning quickly to Luke.*) You what?

(*In the instant that MAC turns, JESSE pulls his gun and points it at MAC. Standoff.*)

JESSE. You're dead, Mac. You've been dead for years. It's time you laid down.

MAC. Jes, what the hell are –

JESSE. Think beyond the room you're in.

LUKE. DADDY!

MAC. The entire military is on red alert waiting for us.

LUKE. I HEARD THE BELL!

MAC. THAT IS *NOT* THE POPSICLE MAN.

JESSE. Let them wait, Mac.

MAC. GODDAMNIT, JES –

JESSE. It's their turn to wait.

MAC. – WE'VE GOT THE FORCE RIGHT THERE IN OUR HANDS.

MR. ANDERSON. (*Hands YOU the umbrella.*) Who knows, you may be that lucky person.

(*The SIREN continues to build. MAC and JESSE remain in their standoff: one hand holding*

the key in their console, the other hand
holding the gun trained on his partner.
All LIGHTS, with the exception of a small shaft of
LIGHT on YOU, and a small shaft of LIGHT
on LUKE, go slowly to BLACK during the
following.)

LUKE. The following is a test of the ... a test of
the ... a test of the time is currently oh forty-nine
... the forecast calls for ... calls four five six
seven times seven is forty-nine was a very good
year ... it was a very good year for small town
girls of independent means the state of not being
dependent ... the state of not being Delaware
Tupperware Anywhere ... turn your radio down
... turn it down ... we interrupt this program to
bring you a glass of water ... a glass of water ... a
glass of what are you gonna do and how're you
gonna keep 'em down on the farm once they've
seen James Dean ... don't adjust your set it down
and don't adjust your set it up and don't adjust
your senses ... just let it be ... whisper words of
wisdom ... let it be or not to be ... just answer the
question and hand me that shovel ... there is a
special providence in Rhode Island ... there is a
sparrow falling in and out of love is a many
splendored thing dedicated to the proposition that
all time held me green and dying though I sang
in my chains like the sea Spot see Spot run away
with the now until the end of time is ...

(*The only lights are now the LIGHTS on YOU and LUKE.*)

LUKE. ... is ... is ... arbitrary ... is ... is ... is ... arm and hammer ... is ... is ... is ...

(*A single GUNSHOT is heard. The LIGHT on Luke snaps out. The SIREN stops, abruptly. Only YOU are lit.*)

YOU.
YOU hear a sort of pause.
YOU feel you've forgotten something.
YOU feel you've left
the stove on
the cat out
the motor running
the phone off the hook.

YOU fear you are destined to die
in a gaggle of near strangers
at happy hour
in the neon of a fern bar.

YOU remember your first kiss but forget your first name.
YOU left so many options open that it rained in your house.
YOU never drove through New England.

YOU left that

book on the coffee table
that
photo on the dresser
that
shirt of hers on the bed.

(*MR. ANDERSON, dressed all in white as the Popsicle Man, rides across the stage on a bicycle. A SPOTLIGHT follows him. HE rings his BELL. HE smiles. HE waves, gracefully. On the handlebars of his bicycle is a box that reads:* POPSICLES, 5¢.

MR. ANDERSON is gone. The SPOTLIGHT goes out. The sound of the BELL fades.

Silence.)

YOU. As YOU hear nothing, and as YOU do nothing – the light on YOU goes to black.

(*IT does.*)

END OF PLAY

As indicated in the text of FOOLIN' AROUND WITH INFINITY, the following program note should be printed and distributed to the audience in their program for the play: (NOTE: The program note will contain writing not found in the text of the play.)

FOOLIN' AROUND WITH INFINITY

A Note from the Playwright

I had read about these guys. The keepers of the keys. Having a preoccupation with people of bizarre occupations, I did what I always do – I started a file. The chain of command – from my President giving the order to deploy the nuclear arsenal, to the commander and his deputy in the silo who turns the keys – was so wonderfully cryptic and Byzantine to me. It had the secret code and handshake feeling of a child's game. It was men playing at war. The file began to fill up.

Into this file went the comment of former Assistant Secretary of Defense Martin Halperin: 'The NATO doctrine is that we will fight with conventional forces until we are losing, then we will fight with tactical nuclear weapons until we are losing, and then we will blow up the world.'

Also into this file went the words of the Pentagon's T.K. Jones regarding how to protect oneself from nuclear fallout: "Dig a hole. Cover it with two doors. Pile three feet of dirt on top. It's the dirt that does it."

In the summer of '82 I began working on a collaborative theatre piece called *Survive*. I worked in a sort of 'dueling playwrights' style with another Minneapolis playwright, David Erickson. David invented a character based entirely on Law and Order. To counter him, I invented a character based on Free Will. Instinct. Zen in overdrive. This character became a young woman. I named her Luke. David and I sat at two typewriters across a kitchen table and proceeded to have a war of language. I remember thinking that our major artistic achievement was the execution of the most perfect cup of Mocha Java coffee I'd ever had. Beyond that, we were stuck. We decided that we needed a specific environment in which our characters could duel. I suggested a Fallout Shelter (I had a file on that, too), and after another magnificent cup of coffee, we lit out on a field trip.

David and I arrived at the Minneapolis Office of Civil Defense, recently placed under the jurisdiction of the Federal Emergency Management Agency (*FEMA*) by the Reagan administration. The building was an old firehouse which had been converted to offices. It was filled with old furniture and new brochures.

A man greeted us. He wore glasses and an old cardigan sweater and looked like my Uncle Al. He was the only employee in sight, and he was thrilled to talk to us. It was clear that having people come to his office interested in Civil Defense was a new and exciting experience for him. This was, after all, the "if-it-happens-it-happens-80's" and not the "prepare-for-the-worst-50's." He shook our hands. He gave us Maxwell House in styrofoam cups. He gave us very specific information on safety procedures during floods, hurricanes and tornadoes. I asked about protection from nuclear fallout. His hand tightened around his styrofoam cup. "We're a lot more prepared for a tornado, *that* I can tell you." Are the shelters safe? Are they stocked with supplies? "Follow me," he said, leading us into the basement of the building. Above a doorway was the familiar black and yellow Fallout Shelter insignia. The room was like a concrete shoebox. Dark and damp. Against one wall was a huge stack of boxes. "Those boxes there. Those're your supplies. Food, water, first aid, radiation detection kits, other stuff. You could go a couple weeks down here if you had to." I was impressed. I mentioned that it looked like an awful lot of boxes to contain only two weeks of supplies. He pulled two of the boxes away from the rest. "These belong down here. The others are for the rest of the city." Pardon me? "They've been here since '71. We just never got 'em distributed. That's why there's so many here." So, all the other shelters are empty? He nodded. "The Federal Emergency Management Agency has yet to determine whether – in the unlikely event of nuclear war – the populace should be housed in the existing shelters within the city, or be transported by bus or train to one huge shelter in the countryside. As soon as this is determined, the appropriate shelters will be stocked."

We drove home in silence. SURVIVE was performed once, then disappeared. David moved to New York. I put Luke in a file.

Several years passed.

I was in a Minneapolis church listening to Helen Caldicott give a lecture on the medical effects of nuclear war. She spoke eloquently, without emotion, for an hour. She spoke clinically about the earth as a patient affected with nuclear fallout as a disease. She was factual, brutal and persuasive. Then, in the last line of her speech, she said: "And finally, I am a mother with children. And let me tell you this: *nobody* harms my kids."

This moment was followed, weeks later, by an event that seemed somehow perfectly related. My President, unaware that a radio mike was on, made a joke. "My fellow Americans, I'm pleased to tell you today that I've signed legislation that will outlaw Russia forever. We begin bombing in five minutes." That same year Vice President George Bush said "Some people believe there can be no such thing as a winner in a nuclear war. But I don't believe that."

My generation – the kids who had crawled under their desks during Civil Defense drills in elementary school – had now, as adults, elected a man who named the MX missile the "Peacekeeper." The unthinkable had become the commonplace. These events made the image of the men in the missile silo return to me. The image of Luke – a human antenna bombarded by the Information Age – returned to me as well. I opened the two files. I introduced them. They seemed to have a lot in common.

We are hounded now by technology that, like Mr. Anderson, will not go away. We attempt futuristic solutions to primitive problems. We cherish laughter and look extinction in the eye. We are playing Frisbee in the graveyard. INFINITY is the collision of these images. Humorous and haunting. Tactile and ephemeral. Infinity continues to look to us all.

COSTUME PLOT

MAC

Act I - Military uniform – dark blue pants, shirt and tie. Decorations befitting rank. "U.S. Air Force" above left shirt pocket. Last name above right shirt pocket. Dark blue (baseball style) cap inscribed with "U.S. Air Force." Black socks and shoes.

Act II - Same.

JESSE

Act I - Military uniform identical to Mac's – but disheveled.

Act II - Same uniform – clean and neatly pressed, military issue overcoat.

LUKE

Act I - Black cotton pants, sleeveless t-shirt, dark loose-fitting shirt (unbuttoned), boots.
Glasses for McPerson moments (preset on down right table). Military uniform identical tc Mac and Jesse's – oversized, fake mustache.

Act II - Add leather bomber jacket (old and worn) to basic look.

MR. ANDERSON

Act I - Popsicle Man – white pants, white shirt, white bow tie, white shoes, white paper "soda jerk" hat.
Traveling Salesman – 1940's style suit, bright print tie, fedora, dark shoes.
Walk-A-Pet Man – bright orange jumpsuit with "Mr. Anderson's Walk-A-Pet" logo on back, orange hat, boots with plastic bags around them as a protective measure.
F.E.M.A. Man – brown pants, light shirt, brown/green cardigan sweater, small bow tie, glasses, construction helmet with Fallout Shelter insignia on front, dark shoes.
Hippie Renter – long tie-dyed robe (must mask dark dress shoes), beads, very long and wild wig, bandana around head.
Conservative Renter (underneath Hippie clothes) – dark blue three-piece suit, white shirt, yellow tie with blue dots, small American flag in breast pocket.

Act II - F.E.M.A. Man – same as Act I.
Brady – military uniform identical to Mac and Jesse's, mustache.
Trick or Treater – dark pants, black sweatshirt, oversized bear mask.

Umbrella Man — very tattered black trenchcoat with "Mr. Anderson's Umbrellas" crudely spray-painted on back, dirty gloves, torn knit cap, old rubber boots, tattered black umbrella.

YOU

Act I - Casual theatre-going garb.

Act II - Same.

PROPERTY LIST

Preset, Act I: Monopoly game (in progress), Speaker phone, Glass of white wine, Military issue handguns in holsters (Mac, Jesse), Quaker Oats box (with 10 neckties inside)

Act I:

Program of the production (YOU, presented by Usher)

2 combination locks

2 military issue pens

Briefcase (with smaller, identical briefcase inside)

Small cloth leash

Heavy leather leash with studs

Miniature straitjacket

Litter bag (inscribed: "Mr. Anderson's Walk-A-Pet"

White bicycle (with small bicycle bell attached)

2 large black notebooks

Tie for Jesse (Dark blue, identical to Mac's)

Cards containing code words (inside smaller briefcase)

Typical leather leash

1 pair of handcuffs

Large handgun

Clipboard with papers

Styrofoam cup of coffee	Pack of gum (Mac)
Newspaper	Small yellow comb
Bottle of scotch	Playboy magazine

Preset, Act II: Monopoly game (in progress), Speaker phone, Glass of white wine, Military issue handguns (Mac, Jesse), Quaker Oats box, bottle of scotch, 2 large black notebooks (at consoles), 2 combination locks (attached to red safe), Program of the production (Luke, inside quaker Oats box), Program of the production (Jesse, inside his large black notebook), 2 keys (inside red safe), Authenticator card (3x5, inside red safe).

Act II:

Package of Certs	2 one dollar bills
Small shovel	5x7 manilla folder
10 instruction cards (inside folder)	Pack of gum (Jesse)
White tie	Credit card (MasterCard)
Military issue handgun (Mr. Anderson as Brady)	Boston fern
Bear mask	Soviet flag
Plastic Halloween pumpkin	Deflated football (will be inflated)